# What Don't Kill Us Makes Us Stronger

## *New Critical Viewpoints on Society Series*
### EDITED BY JOE R. FEAGIN

*What Don't Kill Us Makes Us Stronger: African American Women and Suicide*
By Kamesha Spates (2014)

*Latinos Facing Racism: Discrimination, Resistance, and Endurance*
By Joe Feagin & José A. Cobas (2014)

*Mythologizing Black Women: Unveiling White Men's Racist and Sexist Deep Frame*
By Brittany C. Slatton (2014)

*Diverse Administrators in Peril: The New Indentured Class in Higher Education*
By Edna Chun and Alvin Evans (2011)

# WHAT DON'T KILL US MAKES US STRONGER
## AFRICAN AMERICAN WOMEN AND SUICIDE

### KAMESHA SPATES

Paradigm Publishers
Boulder • London

All rights reserved. No part of the publication may be transmitted or reproduced in any media or form, including electronic, mechanical, photocopy, recording, or informational storage and retrieval systems, without the express written consent of the publisher.

Copyright © 2015 Paradigm Publishers

Published in the United States by Paradigm Publishers, 5589 Arapahoe Avenue, Boulder, CO 80303 USA.

Paradigm Publishers is the trade name of Birkenkamp & Company, LLC, Dean Birkenkamp, President and Publisher.

Library of Congress Cataloging-in-Publication Data

Spates, Kamesha.
  What don't kill us makes us stronger : African American women and suicide / Kamesha Spates.
    pages cm.—(New critical viewpoints on society series)
  Includes bibliographical references and index.
  ISBN 978-1-61205-041-6 (hardcover : alk. paper) —
  ISBN 978-1-61205-223-6 (library ebook) —
  1. African American women—Suicidal behavior.  2. African American women—Psychology.  3. African Americans—Suicidal behavior.  4. Suicide—United States.  I. Title.
  HV6548.U5S63 2014
  362.28082'0973—dc23
                                                    2014026401

Printed and bound in the United States of America on acid-free paper that meets the standards of the American National Standard for Permanence of Paper for Printed Library Materials.

19 18 17 16 15   1 2 3 4 5

*I dedicate this manuscript to my ancestors who fought and died so that I could have the opportunities presented to me today. Additionally, the participants of this study shared very personal details of their lives and I dedicate this project to them. Thank you for sharing your take on this critically important topic. I hope that the accounts shared in this book will aid us in furthering our discussions of suicide in the black community.*

# Contents

| | | |
|---|---|---|
| *Foreword* | | *ix* |
| *Acknowledgments* | | *xv* |
| Chapter 1 | Introduction to the Black-White Suicide Paradox | 1 |
| Chapter 2 | Not All Peaches and Cream: Contemporary Pressures on Black Women | 21 |
| Chapter 3 | I Give All the Glory: The Role of Faith in Black Women's Perceptions of Suicide | 43 |
| Chapter 4 | Survival through Interdependence: Family, Community, and Perceptions of Suicide | 63 |
| Chapter 5 | Only the Strong Survive: Notions of Strength, Resiliency, and Suicide | 83 |
| Chapter 6 | Conclusion: What We've Learned from Black Women about the Suicide Paradox | 105 |
| *Notes* | | *117* |
| *Index* | | *135* |
| *About the Author* | | *140* |

# FOREWORD

Outside of black communities, scholarly and popular commentary about black women often accents a negative type of "black exceptionalism," with an emphasis on pathologies or depressing inequalities. White analysts frequently emphasize negative features of black women's lives that these analysts blame on supposedly weak character or cultural inferiority. The racially stereotyped framing of black personalities, lives, and culture has a long history, even among liberal white social scientists. For instance, the famous analysis of the Jim Crow era, Gunnar Myrdal's *An American Dilemma* (1944), argued that "Negro culture" is "a distorted development, or a pathological condition." Major features of this allegedly pathological culture included family instability, community disorganization, and eccentric religions.[1] Such racially stereotyped framing has persisted in many areas of white America. Many contemporary white analysts continue to insist on a supposed lack of positive black personality, family, and cultural characteristics.

In a brilliant 1940s response to analysts like Myrdal, the great American novelist, Ralph Ellison, countered that black Americans have much that is positive in their values and culture, and much to offer the country:

> Myrdal . . . assumes that "it is to the advantage of American Negroes as individuals and as a group to become assimilated into American culture, to acquire the traits held in esteem by the dominant white Americans."

> ... Which, aside from implying that Negro culture is not also American, assumes that Negroes should desire nothing better than what whites consider highest. But in the "pragmatic sense" lynching and Hollywood, fadism and radio advertising are products of the "higher" culture, and the Negro might ask, "Why, if my culture is pathological, must I exchange it for these?" It does not occur to Myrdal that many of the Negro cultural manifestations which he considers merely reflective might also embody a rejection of what he considers "higher [white] values."[2]

Ellison concludes that in black American culture there is much "of great value and richness, which, because it has been secreted by living and has made their lives more meaningful, Negroes will not willingly disregard."

The interview data and innovative analysis provided here by Kamesha Spates provide much evidence for Ellison's penetrating conclusions. Spates's probing interviews demonstrate well what might be termed positive black exceptionalism—that is, the many positive and admirable characteristics of black women, including their essential contributions to black families and communities. Demonstrably, these African American women are strong in the social arenas that most Americans have long cherished—personal resilience, family, religion, friendships, and community commitments. These remarkable women, like their ancestors, have not only held themselves, their families, and their communities together under difficult racial conditions but also, in reality, have provided much important support for the core institutions of the larger society.

Indeed, the savvy and experienced commentaries of Spates's nearly three dozen interviewees across the United States make evident what insightful black commentators have asserted for centuries now, that this country has never really had a "black problem"—the common white framing of the black situation—but rather has had a "white problem," that is, one of foundational, extensive, and systemic white racism. For centuries one major cost imposed on black women, men, and children by systemic racism is its concealing of much truth about the many admirable aspects of black lives and societal contributions. Spates demonstrates numerous facets of this positive black exceptionalism, but I can only highlight a few key findings in this foreword.

Spates raises the important issue of why the suicide rates for black women are so much lower than for white men and women, a rather surprising empirical reality given this country's hoary and continuing racism. She pursues throughout this book what she terms the black-white suicide paradox, which she summarizes thus: "Why wouldn't black women's suicide rate surpass those of whites when year after year I have seen my mother, sisters, aunts, and female cousins endure multiple stressors? Logically, one would think that black women's suicide rate would surpass white men's, and certainly white women's." Surprisingly, given how easy these striking data on US suicide rates are to find, the extant social science literature does not provide an adequate answer to this important question.

Spates directly confronts key aspects of the black-white suicide paradox and provides some perceptive answers. One aspect is the great array of racially related stressors in black women's everyday environments. As she shows, these painful and recurring stressors should make them more suicide prone than whites, yet they do not. One reason for this is black spirituality and religion. In their racially framed notions about black Americans generally and black women in particular, most whites, including social scientists like Myrdal, ignore the great and meaningful spirituality that is at the heart of African American religion. Yet, as Spates shows, black women's deep spirituality and religious faith provide one important explanation for the very low black female suicide rate—indeed for the fact that a substantial majority of these black female respondents have never entertained even the thought of suicide. Most of these respondents themselves cite early religious upbringing, being taught suicide is a sinful act, and having a spiritual goal of seeking God's purpose in life as likely reasons for that low suicide rate. Indeed, given the very high white male suicide rate, one has to wonder about whether frequent white male claims of being religious, especially in political rhetoric, are actually a true picture of their religion. Interestingly and significantly, Spates's respondents raise serious questions about the character and strengths of white men.

In 1965 an important government report titled *The Negro Family* (the "Moynihan Report") argued that black families and communities are substantially disorganized and pathological, with too few real family and friendship ties and crumbling community relationships.[3] Since that time major magazines and scholarly journals have periodically published articles accenting some version of this white-framed perspective on the allegedly deficient family and other social ties of much of black America. In contrast, Spates finds that her respondents have important social networks that also help to account for the black-white suicide paradox. Her data refute much mainstream analysis in the tradition of the "Moynihan Report." For the most part, the black women's connectedness with family and friends is strong. These family and friendship networks are considered essential. There is, as Spates puts it, a "fundamental and unwavering sense of devotion of these women to their family and friends," and this is reciprocated. The respondents are also active in community activities, including church activities. Their sturdy social networks provide the major and continuing support systems that have many everyday advantages and make even thoughts of suicide highly unlikely. As some respondents put it, "I couldn't kill myself because my family needs me" and "I have committed to helping them, so leaving them is not an option."

Closely linked to their deep spirituality and important social networks is the reality that Spates's interviewees overwhelmingly believe in the strengths of black women, and they provide life narratives that explain this viewpoint. They are very aware that their sustaining and constructive values and culture have been greatly shaped by centuries of struggle with white oppression. One result of dealing constantly with the myriad painful aspects of racial oppression and related life difficulties is the creation of much strength of personal character, purpose, and resiliency—virtues that white America has studiously worked to ignore or misrepresent in favor of antiblack stereotyping. Indeed, in the view of the respondents these important human abilities are often much weaker among whites, especially white men, who have not faced such extensive social and racialized barriers and life trials. These respondents see this strength of character and purpose as part of their communal responsibility as black women, and yet another important reason for the low suicide rate. As Spates puts it, their philosophy of black strength even "seems to neutralize thoughts of suicide."

What then are the main strategies African American women use to stay sane in the face of much racialized insanity that is imposed on them by whites? Spates concludes that the low rate of suicide stems from these important personal and community factors operating together: spirituality and faith, family/friend and community networks, and a strong belief in black women's strengths, including knowing how to manage the long-term racial struggle imposed on them.

It probably has never occurred to most white men, especially those with significant societal power, that their behavior or orientation in regard to suicide (especially their very high suicide rate) and their orientations on some other important matters might be viewed as weak by anyone. Yet, these African American women view the white men they observe as often weak because they are self-centered in their unjustified white privilege and because they have not been tested constantly by the oppressive stressors most black Americans face. As a result, they have not matured to the level of strength and resiliency necessarily developed by black women. In her conclusion Spates puts this point about how they view white men eloquently:

> They perceive both lack of struggle and white privilege to breed weakness and suicidal tendencies. The narratives also revealed that black women perceive suicide as an act of whiteness and thereby of weakness. These perceptions were glaringly negative, and black women used this as an opportunity to define themselves and distance themselves from the thought of suicide.

In my considered view it is long past time for white Americans to give African American women the great credit they deserve for their huge contributions to building up and preserving their families and communities, and indeed this country, over long and painful centuries of racial oppression, to the present day.

*Joe R. Feagin*
*Texas A&M University*

# Acknowledgments

Those who really know me and my story know very much what this accomplishment means to me and my immediate family. To my colleagues, Doctors Joe Feagin, Edward Murguia, Susan Calhoun-Stuber, Penny Green, Brittany Slatton, and Carla Goar, I thank you for your unyielding encouragement and support. To my sisters, Marla, Saniqua, and Brandy, and to my brother, Isaac, I am convinced that your presence in my life is not accidental. I hope that I have been as supportive for you as you have been for me. Thank you for your words of encouragement on a weekly and sometimes daily basis. You know you have friends when they can interpret your sighs. Family, thank you for patience and understanding—I know that I have been difficult to get a hold of lately, but thank you for discerning my heart despite my actions. Granny and Uncle Roy, no words can express the way that I feel about you. You are my guardian angels. You saw something in me early on and your investments in my life have been invaluable. You understood very well that one's life circumstance does not decide one's destiny. Last but not least, to my husband, Elbert, you constantly push me to be a better woman and scholar. Thank you for allowing me to spread myself so thin over the past few years. Although unfair to you, you always saw the bigger picture. Thank you, GOD!

# Chapter 1
# Introduction to the Black-White Suicide Paradox

> *Of the Major Causes of death in the United States, suicide is the only one for which the rates are incontestably lower for blacks than for whites. Herein lies one of the great puzzles for psychiatrists, epidemiologists, and social scientists. If ever there were a group for whom all of the usual concomitants of high suicide rates were present, it would surely be American blacks.*[1]

It was a chilly Texas afternoon approaching the end of the fall 2006 semester when I sat down to have a conversation with one of my colleagues. We discussed politics, specifics about the doctoral program, and suicide. I do not recall exactly how the conversation moved to such an unrelated topic, but I do remember my colleague informing me of some interesting statistics. He took out a piece of paper and wrote down the following numbers: 19.6, 9.6, 5.0, and 1.9 per 100,000.

He then told me that what he had written were the most recent suicide rates for black and white males and females in the United States. Not knowing which rates belonged to whom, I frankly stated that I was not sure which numbers represented which group, but I was certain that black women's suicide rate was the lowest of the four. He assured me that my assumption was correct. I wondered how I knew that. How was I able to assertively provide an answer about something that I have had few encounters with? In all my years as a black woman, I could not remember having had even one conversation with another African American about suicide. Since suicide occurrences are rare in the black community, it is just not a topic of everyday conversation. Even so, I was confident that I could shed light on this phenomenon.

Following this encounter with my colleague, I could not get the idea of black women's low suicide rate out of my mind. After a few weeks of pondering the subject, I began to fully grasp just how inexplicable it was that black women's suicide rate was so low. One question continually confronted me as I considered the ironies: *Why wouldn't black women's suicide rate surpass those of whites when year after year I have seen my mother, sisters, aunts, and female cousins endure multiple stressors? Logically, one would think that black women's suicide rate would surpass white men's, and certainly white women's.*

Shortly after that, I began to search the literature on the subject of the black-white suicide paradox. I discovered that studies investigating this phenomenon are often inconclusive, and are infrequent.[2] I did find, however, that the literature does reach a noteworthy consensus. Numerous scholars of suicide have sounded the call for scientific inquiry on the matter. Specifically, they argue that the scientific community must concentrate its efforts on addressing areas of knowledge scarcity in the suicide literature, particularly concerning other racial and gender groups.[3]

One area for which suicide knowledge is extremely limited is the African American community. This shortage of existing scientific knowledge is further intensified with regard to African American women and suicide. Of four primary subgroups—white males, black males, white females, and black females—the latter group, black females, has (and has always had) the lowest rate of suicide.[4] However, there is little insight as to why this is the case. Consequently, within the suicide literature there has been a recent surge in curiosity regarding the paradoxical relationship between suicide and African American women.

This was all of the confirmation that I needed. I committed myself to this project. I committed myself to allowing black women the opportunity to shed light on this seemingly paradoxical phenomenon by speaking with them in depth about this subject. I needed their stories. More importantly, the literature needed their stories. The identification of this paradox and the scientific call of duty were the direct causes for the emergence of this project.

Low suicide-completion rates deter many researchers from exploring this topic because they assume that nonfatal behavior among this group is also infrequent. Recent pleas from the scientific community claim that nonwhite suicide has gone overlooked far too long. Thus, it is imperative to explore and expand available knowledge concerning black women and the suicide paradox. Previous texts have examined the suicide paradox with regard to the black community in its entirety.[5] However, the purpose of this book is to address a critical gap in the literature. I will explore black women's perceptions concerning their low rate of suicide. A central question remains: why has black women's suicide rate remained low? Therefore, this study is unique in its efforts to concentrate exclusively on black women's perceptions of the suicide paradox.

## Prevalence of Suicide among Black Women

Every 16.2 minutes, a person dies from suicide in the United States. Suicide is the eleventh leading cause of US deaths (with homicide ranking fifteenth) and the third leading cause of death among youth ages fifteen to twenty-four.[6] Suicide affects individuals from all backgrounds and socioeconomic statuses.

In 2000, women and girls made up almost 51 percent of the total US population. Women of color made up nearly half of all US women. Among women of color, black women constituted the largest racial/ethnic group in 2000.[7] Black women certainly face a great many personal and collective challenges; however, their rate of suicide occurrence is noticeably lower than the rate for their male and nonwhite counterparts.

Epidemiological data on persons eighteen years of age and older reveal that African Americans completed 1,954 suicides in 2006. Eighty-five percent were male; this comprises a rate of 8.8 per 100,000. African American females' suicide statistics reported a rate of 1.4 per 100,000. The ratio of African American male to female suicides is 5.85 to 1.[8]

Dating back several decades, African American women's suicide rates have remained virtually nonexistent. In fact, suicide statistics among black women have changed little in fifty years. As of 2006, the age-adjusted suicide rate for black women was 1.4 per 100,000, compared to their 1950 rate of 1.8 per 100,000. Their rate peaked at 2.5 (a total of 343) per 100,000 and has not surpassed 2.0 per 100,000 since 1981.[9]

Statistics confirm that black women have the lowest suicide rate of all racial/ethnic groups. Recent suicide statistics reveal that black women's rate is 9.4 times lower than the national average (13.2 per 100,000), while white women's rate is approximately 2.2 (6.1 per 100,000) times lower than the national average and white men's rate is 1.5 times above the national average at 19.6 per 100,000.[10]

A recent study concluded that along with having the lowest suicide rate, black women also have the narrowest age distribution for suicidal behavior, ranging from early twenties to mid-forties. This study showed that virtually no suicides occurred outside this window for black women. This same study noted that the mean age of white suicide victims was 46.2 and the mean age of black suicide victims was 36.8. These findings indicate that not only do blacks commit suicide less often than do whites, but on average they tend to commit suicide much earlier in life.[11]

When considering white males and females, higher suicide rates tend to be reported among those with fewer than twelve years of education. For blacks, those between the ages of twenty-five and fifty-four with lower levels of education are more likely to commit suicide. However, older blacks differ from older whites in that lower educational attainment seems to have no effect on their risk for suicide.[12]

## Suicide Attempts

An examination of differences in the rates of suicide attempts among all males and females divulges critical differences in the literature. For every completed suicide, there are twenty-five attempts. Generally, females are more likely to attempt suicide than males. In 2006 the ratio of female to male attempts was nearly three to one. Patterns in completion rates show that men are four times more likely to die from suicide than women. So, even though women attempt suicide more often than men, men's attempts are more lethal.[13]

A further breakdown by race and gender reveals that the rate of attempted suicide for white females is significantly higher than that for black females.[14] Even though the literature suggests that nonfatal suicide statistics are not documented nearly to the extent of fatal suicide attempts, it's still evident that white women attempt suicide more frequently than their black counterparts.[15] For instance, in 2008, 19,560 black women attempted suicide, compared to 137,694 white women.[16] These figures verify a seven-to-one ratio of suicide attempts by white and black females.

## Why Black Women's Suicide Rates Puzzle Social Scientists

To fully comprehend discussions of black women within the suicide literature, it is imperative that we address the complexities surrounding black women's social position in the United States. Black women's subordinate status is amplified by occupying dual roles as racial and gender minorities. The literature suggests that black women's social standing, alongside their distinct cultural dynamics, is critical to discussions of why their suicide rate has remained so low.[17] Since black women's suicide rate is significantly lower than that of any other group, their unique cultural dynamics deserve attention. These discussions will later serve as a point of reference to evaluate whether the suicide literature acknowledges black women's unique social position.

The social-science literature clearly illustrates the unique oppressive conditions of black women in America.[18] As already mentioned, black women suffer greater economic, educational, and health challenges than whites, yet their rate of suicide is significantly lower. Given the risk factors for suicide, we might expect blacks to be just as suicide prone as (if not more so than) whites. The literature refers to these inconsistencies as the suicide paradox—the exception to unfavorable racial health disparities.[19]

### Health and Social Disparities

The literature reveals that black women at every income level are disproportionately affected by health disparities. Heart disease and cancer are leading causes of death for all women. However, black women are almost

50 percent more likely to die from cancer than white women and 33 percent more likely to die from heart disease.[20] Perceptions of ill health appear to be more prevalent among black women than white women. According to the Medical Expenditure Panel Survey, 20.5 percent of black women compared to 13.4 percent of white women classify themselves as being in fair or poor health.[21]

The life expectancy of whites exceeds that of blacks at every income level. Women of all racial and ethnic backgrounds have a greater life expectancy than men. However, black women have the lowest life expectancy of all US women: 74.3 years compared to 80.5 for white women.[22]

Black women also tend to have a higher poverty rate. In 1998 nearly 51 percent of black women were living near or below the poverty level, compared to 25 percent of white women.[23] Wealth and income disparities play a major role in explaining why both black women and their children are disproportionately affected by poverty.[24] A great number of black households with children under the age of eighteen are headed by black women.[25] Evidence suggests that an increasing resistance among black women to "marry down," coupled with a shortage of available black men, is negatively altering the poverty dynamic of the black community.[26]

Educational attainment is among the key indicators used to determine socioeconomic status and thereby predict the likelihood of a lifetime of poverty. Black women significantly lag in this area as well. Black women's educational attainment is nearly half that of their white counterparts. Only 22.3 percent of black women in the United States hold a bachelor's degree or higher, compared to 34.4 percent of white women.[27] This can prove to be a significant setback over the course of a lifetime. The median income for those with a bachelor's degree is approximately 74 percent higher than the median income for those with only a high-school diploma.[28]

## Mental Health

Black women's mental-health statistics mirror their physical-health statistics. They have been identified as a high-risk group for depression. Medical practitioners have also identified black women as less likely to seek treatment for their illnesses.[29] Black women's hesitance to get treatment for depression makes this a complex issue to address. Instead of seeking treatment, many opt to cope with depression by overachieving, overeating, or obsessing about their physical appearance. Researchers have argued that compulsive eating may be a culturally acceptable way to "speak the unspeakable."[30]

In her article "Stress More Crippling in Black Women Than White Counterparts," Talise D. Moorer revealed substantial differences in the ways that black women and white women handle stress. While white women are more likely to seek social support from others to mend their circumstances, black women are inclined to put their efforts into enduring their conditions rather than trying to solve or alleviate the situation. This same study also exposed racial differences in the likelihood of identifying stressors. Despite being under greater stress, black women are either unaware that they are stressed or are not willing to admit it. As a result, researchers were forced to rely on blood-pressure readings and heart rates to reveal concrete results.[31]

## The African American Experience

Many Africans were brought to the United States and the Caribbean involuntarily. The African American experience begins when approximately twenty Africans were forced ashore by white settlers at the Jamestown colony. Over the next 200 years, thousands of people in Africa were stolen from their homelands, torn away from their families, and subjected to extreme hardship when forced into slavery in the United States.[32]

However, contrary to what many Americans believe, the African migration occurred on several different levels. Some Africans reached North American shores as freemen and others came as indentured servants who fulfilled their duties and went on to live out their lives as freemen.[33] During the seventeenth century the Irish and Africans coexisted as indentured servants. The two groups lived and worked in communal areas, and some even ran away together to form partnerships against their oppressors. Ultimately, growing discontent by Irish and African workers forced white landowners to make a decision. Upper-class, white, male landowners decided to restructure society on the basis of class and race. These actions resulted in a drastic decline in the number of Irish indentured servants. Blacks, on the other hand, could more easily be denied their rights based on the color of their skin and could thus be more easily controlled.[34]

Reconstruction, from the mid-1860s to the late 1870s, was an attempt by the US government to address the return of the Southern states to the Union following the abolishment of slavery.[35] Reconstruction also provided former slaves with equal protection under the law, along with the rights to vote and to receive an education.

During the period of slavery and during Reconstruction and its aftermath, the foundation for many basic American racial attitudes was established. Joe Feagin argues that racial attitudes consisted of a complex array of antiblack practices, the unjustly gained political-economic power of whites, continuing economic and other resource inequalities along racial lines, and white racist ideologies and attitudes to maintain and rationalize white privilege. He claims that this phenomenon later set the foundation for what he refers to as systemic racism.[36]

Although social and economic conditions among African Americans initially improved during Reconstruction, these gains were short-lived. In 1867 Jim Crow laws were ratified. From 1867 until about 1965, and as late as the 1970s in certain places, Jim Crow laws enforced the "separate but equal" doctrine. Although this set of guidelines was originally created with blacks in mind, other groups of color were at times held to these strict rules.[37]

Consequently, in the United States we have a group of individuals who *technically* have been free from legal restrictions and lawfully protected for fifty years at most. As one might imagine, these circumstances continue to pose challenges in the contemporary lives of black families.

## Consequences of Racial and Gender Oppression

Contemporary black women are further distraught by the unique stressors that they face due to racism and sexism in the United States. Associated consequences of oppressive realities certainly deserve more attention.[38] Nonetheless, evidence suggests that there are direct correlations between racism, racial life events, and poor mental health. For instance, ethnic minorities are less likely to report race-related crime incidents to authorities, and psychologists are more likely to ignore the impact of race-related encounters on minority victims.[39]

Stereotyping and racial prejudice are connected to much more negative cultural and social outcomes. They can perpetuate visual images of a group that are damaging at virtually every level.[40] Prejudices, stereotyping, and cultural rejection at the individual and institutional levels can thereby lead to additional stress. This phenomenon is further exacerbated among black women in that they have faced physical, moral, and spiritual stigmatization to a greater degree. Racial and gender hierarchies that pervade the American social consciousness compel many to perceive contemporary black women's social worth as subordinate to that of other groups.

Racism and discrimination evoke feelings of powerlessness among black women. Black women convey that their bouts with racism are often presented by race scholars as secondary to black men's or white women's problems.[41] Misrepresentations of black women through racial stereotypes have resulted in daunting mistreatment of them. Portrayals of black women as overbearing or as sex-crazed jezebels mirror the ideologies connected to the various structures that shape our society.[42]

Continuous exposure to oppressive conditions has debilitating psychological effects on people of color and even more so on women of color.[43] The severity of the oppression that black women have encountered has forced them to reinvent themselves.[44] Facing multiple forms of discrimination at once is a daily struggle for the contemporary black woman. Unlike their counterparts, black men and white women, black women must deal with the fact that their femaleness and blackness are interlocking identities; thus, it is impossible for them to escape their twofold character.[45]

## Theoretical Explanations of Racial Differences in Suicide

Very few theoretical works address racial or gender variations in US suicide rates. Some contemporary explanations apply traditional explanations to black suicide without considering how cultural distinctions impact their findings. Standard sociological explanations for the suicide phenomenon derive from Émile Durkheim. His theory of suicide posits that the extent to which a person is socially connected and/or regulated impacts his or her likelihood of suicidal behavior. Suicide is most likely to occur in a society characterized with either low or high levels of social integration or regulation. Cases in which social integration results in excessive individualism or communalism create a recipe for disaster. Likewise, cases in which surroundings result in absolute normlessness or authoritarianism will yield similar consequences. Therefore, societies that maintain moderate levels of social regulation and social integration are likely to have fewer suicides among their members.[46]

Especially important in Durkheim's analysis is the influence of religion. Durkheim argued that religion encourages moderate integration; that is, the formation of a collective life and collective community. Much of contemporary suicide literature preserves this assumption. The literature maintains that being involved in a religious group, partaking in church activities, and belonging to close-knit communities promote social integration. Therefore, religion appears to have a preventive effect on suicide.[47]

Along the same lines, studies have proven that unmarried individuals are at greater risk for suicide.[48] Durkheim found marriage to be a protective factor against suicide for both males and females, but especially among middle-aged and older males. Additional background characteristics reveal that whites are much more likely than African Americans to be married in their lifetime. Specifically, as of 2002, 26 percent of black women ages fifteen to forty-four were married, compared to 51 percent of white women and 41 percent of white men.[49] Black women's low marriage rate is yet another example of the perplexing inconsistencies surrounding the black-white suicide paradox.

Also according to Durkheim's suicide theory, social regulation is an important variable in suicide prediction. Durkheim defined social regulation as the extent to which society controls an individual's attitudes, desires, and emotions, leaving little room for optimism. He referenced African slavery as an example of excessive normative regulation. Normlessness, or too little regulation, occurs in environments in which there are elevated amounts of conflict or little regularity regarding social norms—for instance, societies in which it is fairly simple to obtain a divorce.

Durkheim's suicide theory has received much criticism for its failure to include an in-depth examination of race, culture, or gender in its analysis. Although Durkheim briefly explored notions of increased fatalistic suicidal tendencies among the African slave population, his theory does little else to account for variance in suicide incidents between racial groups. Regarding gender, he briefly attempted to explain the variables that impact gender-specific risks. For instance, he found that although living a single or divorced lifestyle affects both gender groups equally, surviving a spouse's death appears to have a greater impact on males than females. Durkheim claimed that in these instances, widowers (males) have a more difficult time satisfying their needs outside of the family. Females (widows) are able to more easily cope with losing a spouse because they are better able to fulfill familial needs through other means. Durkheim explored varying gender dynamics, yet he failed to provide insight on risk factors associated with women of color.

Though Durkheim's theories on the topic of suicide created a framework for contemporary suicide studies, researchers often criticized the limitations of his studies. Peter Bearman, for instance, argued that Durkheim neglected to mention that in abnormal contexts, integration and regulation are not one and the same. Bearman criticized Durkheim's analysis of the suicide phenomenon by arguing that Durkheim's notions of anomic, fatalistic, altruistic, and egoistic suicides will transpire in only the most ideal circumstances.[50]

Even though Bearman addressed the critical point of structure, he too failed to acknowledge the importance of providing a more in-depth examination of cultural variation within the suicide phenomenon. Chris Girard, however, attempted to establish a more inclusive approach to the study of suicide. He sought to provide readers with a more diverse and accurate examination of risk factors associated with the contemporary suicide phenomenon. He criticized Durkheim's theory of social integration by arguing that it neglected to consider the significance of age and gender. He went on to say that the suicide phenomenon becomes more complicated when one attempts to introduce other variables into the study of this occurrence, such as ascribed and achieved characteristics.[51]

Generally speaking, Girard believed that achievement statuses tend to increase the likelihood of suicidal behavior. Girard argued that since men's roles in US society tend to be centered more on achieved statuses (such as education or income), their suicide rates tend to be higher when they are unable to live up to expectations. Likewise, he claimed that suicide rates among young men exceed those of young women because women's roles in the United States are centered on the family, so young women succumb to societal pressures to marry and to start a family by a certain age. In cases where they are unable to achieve these goals, they too face increased risks of suicide.[52]

Girard, then, provides us with a more comprehensive analysis of what places a person at risk for suicide than did earlier studies, such as those by Durkheim and Bearman. Girard's research considers both structural (social identifications such as age and gender) and cultural (achieved status) dynamics as playing a role in increasing an individual's risk for suicidal behavior. Nevertheless, Girard, too, failed to point out the role of race in his study; thus, the complexity of women of color is absent from his analysis.

Charles Prudhomme developed a theory focused on the association between suicide and modernization.[53] He was one of the first to explore the suicide paradox among African Americans. His groundbreaking analysis attempted to provide insight into why African Americans have lower suicide rates than do whites. He contended that suicide does not affect African Americans to the extent that it affects whites because of social differences between the two groups. Educationally and economically, blacks lag behind whites, so in extreme times of need, such as during the Great Depression, they had far less to lose.

Recognizing the importance of Durkheim's social-integration theory, Prudhomme innovatively highlighted the importance of interpersonal ties in relation to African American suicide rates. He claimed that African Americans appear to better utilize interpersonal ties, placing more of an emphasis on social ties and religion, in comparison to whites. Therefore, black-white economic and education disparities, social integration, and faith-based beliefs safeguard African Americans against factors that traditionally place one at risk for suicidal behavior.[54] Although his analysis addressed a critical gap in the literature, Prudhomme did little to explain gender differences in suicide rates within African American or white communities.

Like Bearman and Girard, Herbert Hendin criticized Durkheim's theory as being too simplistic. He argued that if social disruption is one of the primary causes for suicide, as Durkheim suggested, then rates among the black population should be higher than rates among the white population. He believed that, instead, insight into the black-white suicide paradox lies in group response to rejection and anger.[55]

Long-term bouts of racism and discrimination have better equipped African Americans to manage widespread rejection. Accordingly, they can more easily identify their source of anger. On the other hand, whites have significantly less experience handling these matters and are thereby unsure as to where they should direct their feelings. African Americans turn their rage outward, making them more prone to homicidal behavior. On the contrary, whites are more likely to internalize their rage, hence making them more likely to turn to suicide as a means of coping. Therefore, Hendin concluded that suicidal behavior and homicidal behavior are inversely associated.[56]

Not only did Hendin explore suicide-rate differences among blacks; he also offered uncharted knowledge concerning suicidal black women. Hendin's case studies revealed a noticeable pattern. The majority of black women who made suicide attempts typically did so after experiencing some sort of relationship setback with the opposite sex or issues with maternal abandonment. One participant in his study mentioned that her depressive episodes and suicidal ideations altered depending on her relationship standing with her husband. When things were going well she was delighted, but when conflict arose so too did her suicidal thoughts.

Although Hendin provided insight into the implications of cultural stress that African Americans disproportionately share at the societal level, his work has been criticized for extrapolating his findings about suicidal individuals to nonsuicidal individuals or suicide attempters. Additionally, because all of the women in Hendin's case studies struggled with issues of parental abandonment and significant mistrust of the opposite sex, it is unclear whether Hendin's findings are generalizable to contemporary black women.

Contemporary social scientists concur that the black-white suicide paradox remains perplexing.[57] Theories that focus on between-group rate differences have been unable to provide definitive explanations for this phenomenon. Because black women's accounts of suicide are scarce, scholars recognize the importance of addressing the knowledge gap. Thus, Davor Jedlicka and colleagues asserted almost three decades ago that there were no existing theories to explain racial and/or gender differences in US suicide occurrences.[58] The same statement rings true today.

## Black Women's Tools for Evading Suicide

As discussed earlier, black women experience unique stressors due to racism and sexism in the United States. But again there is a lack of empirically and theoretically based knowledge concerning this phenomenon. The vast majority of the clinical research that has been done tends to study black women from a pathological perspective. The negative mental-health effects caused by issues such as substance abuse, dysfunctional black-family circumstances, single parenthood, and other issues are typically the topic areas of study. However, the ways in which black women respond to their oppressive realities deserve much more attention.[59]

My conversations with black women allowed me insights into some of the most personal areas of their lives. These women spoke in detail about their aversion to suicide and, more importantly, sparked a dialogue unseen in contemporary suicide literature. They centered their discussions on consciously redefining themselves.

The notion of black women redefining themselves is expanded in Patricia Hill Collins's and Deborah Gray White's discussions of black women finding their voice. These researchers claim that the only way in which black women have been able to survive such harsh circumstances is by redefining themselves.[60] Similar findings resonated with my participants. Therefore, regardless of the origins of their stress, black women filtered their experiences through their perceptions of themselves as strong.

According to my respondents, notions of faith-based beliefs, strong historical references, social networks, and a reconstruction of the image of suicide victims as weak were all instruments commonly utilized to create and maintain their perceptions of themselves as survivors. The respondents generally claimed that the origins of these strategies are passed down from preceding generations. Examples ranged from childhood memories to interactions with family and friends. Additionally, respondents derived their strength from the notion of collective memory, which suggests that objects such as pictures or stories about relatives—both living and dead—serve as channels to chronicle past experiences to those in the present.[61]

Therefore, respondents overall perceived the suicide paradox through a racialized lens. Suicide and whiteness were synonymous, just as strength and blackness were one and the same. My study offers personal details surrounding black women's lives. It shares specific strategies concerning the tools the women most often utilized. Such tools appear to be most useful for coping with negative life events and overcoming structural barriers. Therefore, my findings suggest that it is imperative for racial and gender inequities to remain at the forefront of discussions concerning US suicide trends. Existing social structure and sociocultural variation may play a greater role than we think in an individual's decision to end his or her life. Subsequent chapters in this book provide more in-depth analysis of these findings.

## Combining Micro Data with Macro Theory

Michael Burawoy's extended case method guided my methodological course of action. Burawoy's work focuses on making use of existing theory in hopes of understanding one's data.[62] Additionally, this method pays particular attention to the importance of the frameworks of respondents as well as the macro determinants of everyday life. As Burawoy states,

> The *extended case method* applies reflexive science to ethnography in order to extract the general from the unique, to move from the "micro" to the "macro," and to connect the present to the past in anticipation of the future, all by building on preexisting theory.[63]

Rather than neglecting or downplaying the importance of social structure, the extended case method operates on the basis of seeking to unveil how the "social situation" is ultimately shaped by wider structures. Because the suicide literature is well established, it was important to utilize the existing knowledge as a foundation for this study.

I believed that the extended case method would be particularly appropriate for this study because black women's accounts of suicide would provide rich, detailed data without necessitating that I disregard previous suicide literature or contemporary structural conditions pertaining to black women. The extended case method encourages the bringing together of micro data and macro theory. For example, by applying fundamental principles of reflexive science and ethnography, the approach encourages dialogue between us and the people we study. As a result, the insider status of the researcher appears to correspond nicely with this methodological framework.

Black women's narratives are vital to exploring the black-white suicide paradox. Traci West declares that the voices of black women are rarely heard, and when they are their statements frequently are taken out of context. They are considered too emotional and lacking objectivity.[64] Therefore, I was adamant about providing black women a platform to speak for themselves concerning the notion of suicide. This project allowed black women's experiences to illuminate the suicide literature, which to date has been significantly lacking their voices.

This study explores black women's perceptions of the black-white suicide paradox, along with their perceptions of their extremely low suicide rate, through in-depth interviews. This approach is particularly appropriate because rather than conduct a study that would allow generalization, I sought narratives from black women that would provide rich, detailed data. Existing empirical evidence regarding suicide among black women also influenced my decision to opt for semistructured interviews with the women.[65] As a result, insights gained from this study significantly advance the suicide literature with thorough, detailed accounts of black women's perceptions of the paradox. At the same time, this study's findings provide a valuable foundation for future researchers seeking to study the black-white suicide paradox on a much larger scale.

## Black Female Participants

I conducted thirty-three interviews either face-to-face or by telephone with black women ages eighteen and older. The women were also required to have no history of serious mental illness or previous suicide attempts. Thirty-two of the thirty-three respondents self-identified as belonging to the African American racial group. The thirty-third respondent categorized herself as "other" due to her Creole/African background. The participants ranged from eighteen to sixty-eight years of age.

In order to interview women from a wide array of backgrounds, I recruited women from different geographical locations. My initial research participants were recruited through contacts that I had established in the Midwest and South of the United States. All remaining study participants were recruited through email advertisements and word-of-mouth snowballing techniques.[66] Although the sample is nonrandom, I made every possible effort to include a demographically representative sample of the larger population of African American women.

Twenty-four participants had children, leaving nine that did not. In terms of education, all study participants held at least a high-school diploma or GED. Specifically, nine of the women held a high-school diploma or GED, two completed technical school, five had some college, three held bachelor's degrees, and fourteen were in pursuit of a graduate-level degree or had already completed one.

Current relationship statuses of the study participants indicated that more than half of the women (twenty-one, to be exact) were single; eight women were married, three were divorced, and one was widowed. With regard to annual income, nearly half of the respondents reported earning under $29,999 per year, approximately one-third reported earning $30,000–$49,999 per year, and nearly one-fifth reported earning over $50,000 per year. Specific breakdowns are as follows: six reported annual earnings $14,999 or below; nine reported earning $15,000–$29,999; eleven reported earning $30,000–$49,999; four reported earning $50,000–$69,999; and three reported earning more than $100,000 per year.

Religious or faith-based beliefs were a fairly common attribute among the women. For example, twenty-eight classified themselves as Christian, and twenty-one of those reported being active in a local church or religious group. Three identified as Buddhist, one as Muslim, and one as atheist. Interview questions were mostly open-ended. Questions allowed women to speak to a variety of relevant issues in their lives, such as their childhood, personal coping mechanisms for dealing with individual and social stressors, and to what extent the black community's perceptions of suicide have impacted their own.

## Literature-Based Assumptions

The working hypothesis for this study is based on three baseline considerations derived from the literature before data collection began. The first is that black women's religious beliefs are significant in their perceptions of suicide. Studies going back to Durkheim have shown this to be a common factor among populations with low suicide rates. Similar results also emerged in five preliminary unstructured interviews conducted with black women.

The second literature-based assumption is centered on the notion of social networks. According to the literature from Durkheim and others, social integration appears to be fairly well established in the social-science and suicide literature. Therefore, I expected that the study participants would deem social networks essential to the low rates of suicide among black women. This assumption, however, was in direct opposition to some existing studies that have examined the social networks of black women. With pathological portrayals of the black family dominating a significant part of the race literature in the United States, prominent race theorists have argued that many of the black family's social ties and networks have been weakening.[67] If this were true, one would expect an increasing suicide rate among black women. Since this is not the case, we are faced with an apparent contradiction.

The third and final baseline consideration references the multifaceted stressors experienced by contemporary black women. Black women reside in a unique social position in the United States. I theorized that the grueling conditions that have overwhelmed contemporary US African American women have ultimately resulted in the development of various coping strategies that enable them to survive even when faced with the most difficult challenges.[68]

The primary goal of this exploratory study was to interview a diverse sample of African American women about their perceptions of the black-white suicide paradox. In addition to black women's perceptions of the paradox, I gave a great deal of attention to the types of relative individual and social stressors in black women's lives. Individual stressors ranged from issues in their personal relationships and their jobs, to material and financial want, to an array of social stressors such as the impact in their lives of widespread misrepresentations of black women and unrealistic expectations. Significant attention was also given to the types of methods black women credited with maintaining their low suicide rate.

## Synopsis of Chapters

In subsequent chapters I provide an in-depth analysis of the study findings. Chapters 2 through 5 present research findings by way of the reoccurring themes that emerged from in-depth interviews. Chapter 2 presents black women's accounts of their contemporary stressors and highlights the complex linkages between black women's infrequent use of suicide and their current social status. Again, black women would seem to be just as suicide prone—if not more so—than whites, given the risk factors for suicide and the accumulation of stressors that they face. Black women speak candidly about these contemporary stressors.

Chapter 3 explores the notion of religion and faith as an explanation for black women's low suicide rate. According to the US Religious Landscape Survey, black women disproportionately constitute the largest group of Christians.[69] Participants conveyed that their notions of faith, around which their personal decisions to avoid suicide orbited, seemed especially to encompass their respective perceptions of a higher power. This chapter concludes by outlining ways in which religion and faith most likely buffer the risk of suicidal behavior among black women.

Chapter 4 examines the extent to which social networks provide insight into black women's low suicide rate. This chapter offers an up-close look at how these support systems lessen the likelihood of suicidal tendencies among black women. I present the black women's narratives on the multifaceted advantages of belonging to close-knit communities. Accounts presented in this chapter candidly speak to the dynamics of how these support systems operate in relation to the suicide paradox.

Chapter 5 addresses how the vast majority of participants' narratives credited the unique strength of black women as a primary cause for their low suicide rate. This philosophy of strength seems to neutralize thoughts of suicide. This chapter also examines black women's accounts of the origins of their strength along with ways in which this perspective serves as a safeguard against acts of suicide.

Lastly, Chapter 6 offers a comprehensive summary of each theme revealed from black women's narratives regarding their low suicide rate. This chapter also revisits the research purpose and goals in relation to current literature, offers a comprehensive conclusion to the study, and outlines implications for future research.

## Chapter 2
## Not All Peaches and Cream
### Contemporary Pressures on Black Women

*We have social obligations to our immediate family, our community, our churches, to work as well. We have to balance the household as well as our social obligations, which usually doesn't leave much time for us to really take care of ourselves. So, it's the combination of those outside obligations that leads us to not really understand how to help ourselves when those times come.*

—Jennifer[1]

Jennifer, a single black woman, offers an interesting look at the assortment of stressors that black women encounter in contemporary society. Her quote reflects the views expressed by many other black women in this study. The accounts discussed in this chapter speak to black women's recognition of the multifaceted challenges that they endure in their attempts to live balanced lives.

This chapter offers insight into the daily stressors that affect black women. During these discussions black women highlighted prejudice and discrimination, unrealistic expectations, and financial want as significant sources of stress. Nearly all study participants reported that they experienced some form of prejudice and/or discrimination in professional settings, despite their levels of education or income. Additionally, three-fourths of the women deemed prejudice and/or discriminatory actions to be significant sources of stress in their daily lives. Narratives also revealed that these incidents were not limited to the workplace or school, but also occurred at parks, at shopping malls, in their neighborhoods, and in several other locations. Nearly half of the women conveyed that family is a significant source of stress, and one-third of the women believed that financial want constituted a significant stressor in their lives. I conclude this chapter by presenting black women's personal accounts of suicidal ideations and attempts.

## Black Women's State of Affairs

Contemporary literature reveals that blacks continue to face significant hardships. For instance, minorities, particularly blacks, suffer economic, educational, health, and social difficulties to a greater extent than do whites.[2] More specifically, Adalberto Aguirre and Jonathan Turner argue that the legacy of slavery still plagues African Americans today, characterized by disproportionate numbers of single-parent homes, high unemployment rates, and unequal education.[3] The social-science literature clearly illustrates that black women's attempts to navigate these circumstances present them with a distinct set of dilemmas.[4]

A closer look at the current state of African American women's physical, mental, and social circumstances reveals noteworthy disparities.[5] For instance, African American women tend to have a higher poverty rate than white women. In 2012 just over 25 percent of African American women were living below the poverty level, compared to just over 10 percent of white women.[6] The disproportionate poverty rate among African American women has significant consequences for their children.[7] For instance, approximately 38 percent of African American children live in poverty compared to just over 12 percent of white children in the United States.[8]

Black women disproportionately live in female-headed households. More than 40 percent of women heading their own households live below the poverty line.[9] Additionally, female-headed households are less likely to have a member in the labor force, and more likely to experience economic hardship than are male-headed households.[10] In order to survive, black women are frequently charged with being sole income providers and decision makers for the household, and with single-handedly raising children. Therefore, while black men are disproportionately unemployed and incarcerated, African American women are increasingly vital to the survival of the black family.[11]

Due to this current state of affairs African American women are often placed in a position of economic distress.[12] Beyond notions of material want, poverty is also believed to negatively influence one's psychological health. In fact, research confirms a positive correlation between poverty rates and depression.[13] Therefore, since African American women are disproportionately affected by poverty, they may face an increased risk of developing depression compared to their more affluent counterparts.[14]

Race and gender discrimination add an additional layer of complexity to the lives of contemporary black women. The widespread discrimination that black women face can leave them feeling powerless. Black women report that continually battling discrimination at the individual and institutional levels leads to increased stress.[15] Racial and gender hierarchies that pervade US social consciousness compel many Americans to perceive contemporary African American women's social worth as subordinate.

These factors bring us to consideration of the black-white suicide paradox. Black women have a well-recorded history of oppression and discrimination.[16] Remnants of their disenfranchised history remain evident as African Americans continue to suffer economic, educational, and health challenges on a larger scale than whites. Additionally, African Americans endure higher rates of morbidity and mortality than whites, except in the area of suicide.[17] African American women's suicide rate remains a noteworthy exception to these adverse racial health disparities.

Untreated depression is the number-one cause of suicide for African Americans and whites alike.[18] Yet, as mentioned previously, black women's rate of depression equals and in some cases exceeds that of whites. In a world where black women would seem just as prone to suicide as whites, their rate tells a different story. To understand the extent of the paradoxical relationship between black women and their suicide rates, one must closely examine the stressors that black women face, how they perceive these stressors, and ultimately how they cope (which I examine in the chapters that follow). This chapter looks at contemporary black women's stressors. These discussions of stressors allow black women to bring attention to the difficulties that they deem significant and encounter most often. In doing so, the narratives divulge the extent to which social scientists find black women's suicide rate so intriguing: when comparing suicide risk factors with the accumulation of stressors that black women deal with, social scientists agree that black women appear to be a rare exception to the prevailing ideas in the literature.[19]

## Personal Stressors of Black Women

### Mistreatment in Professional Settings

More than two-thirds of the women conveyed in their narratives that they face prejudice and discriminatory acts from whites in public settings. These findings were consistent irrespective of the women's geographical location, income, or education level. These incidents most commonly occurred in settings where there are legal sanctions for racial or gender discrimination (i.e., the workplace or school). The considerable amount of stress that these incidents were causing the women was apparent throughout these discussions. When asked, "What are the existing stressors that you currently face in your life and where do the majorities come from?" a participant named Hilldreth shared this:

> I believe that a major stressor that we [black women] all face is still inequality. We often don't have the resources that we need to accomplish the things that we want to accomplish. They're not made readily available to us as they are to white females, and we know that. Black women, I think, are still looked down upon, and what I mean by that is, for example, if there were four doctors, a white male, a black male, a white female, and a black female, people will probably go to the white male doctor first then the black male, then the white female, then the black female because they think that we're inadequate.

Hilldreth's example of inequality as a source of stress is a very important one. Hilldreth is pursuing a graduate-level degree in nursing with the hopes of one day becoming a nurse practitioner, so her concerns are very much justified. She shared that she is one of the few African Americans in her academic program, and that has been a significant stressor for her. So, we see here that not only is Hilldreth experiencing challenges as an underrepresented minority in her program, but she is also aware of how racism will affect her relationships with her patients once she is practicing in her profession.

Her story of the racism experienced by nonwhite physicians has been noted in the research. For instance, Mana Lumumba-Kasongo, a black female physician, shares accounts of the racism that she has experienced throughout her career. Her patients often question her authority and ability to make treatment decisions and at times patients have outright refused her services until the "real doctor"—a white male—arrives.[20] Hilldreth later revealed that, though she is aware of the difficulties that await her, she refuses to let these stereotypes deter her desire to serve others.

Ceva, a college student, also works at a predominantly white university. She shared her experiences confronting stereotypical attitudes from coworkers on campus:

> Being that you're black and a woman you are considered two steps lower. It's tough, always having to fight to say, "I'm this person. I know what I'm doing!" So you work extra hard. You go the extra mile and you spend a little bit more time at the office. You have to become extra friendly to make sure that they [whites] don't think that you're loud or ghetto. You just do everything possible to make yourself blend in and be accepted as just a person and not the black woman.

She commented that one of her biggest stressors comes from the constant stream of energy that she exudes attempting to ensure that her white coworkers are comfortable with her presence. Ceva's account mirrors Charisse Jones and Kumea Shorter-Gooden's analysis of black women's experience in the workplace. Jones and Shorter-Gooden reveal that black women's attempts to mitigate racism by going above and beyond to appear as team players ultimately causes excess stress.[21]

Study participant Delilah revealed that discrimination in the workplace has also been a major source of stress for her, particularly over the last few years. She reminisced about an event at her place of employment that involved wage discrimination:

> You're hired to do a particular job, and then you do that; but then that's not enough. And when I say that's not enough, you may have a white counterpart who would not be as qualified to do what you do, but would be earning twice what you're earning. But you [the black woman] end up doing the work of her job and somebody else's. Yet, when it comes to pay, your white counterpart would get the bonus or they would go to bat for her instead of you. So yeah [pauses], I have had to deal with that for some time now. And how I did it, I just continued to do my job, and I legally fought it and in the end it paid off. But it took years, and I didn't leave because I liked what I was doing, I loved my job. And I had great benefits. So now it's a lot better. But I went through a period there where it wasn't, and I could easily have walked out.

As Delilah mentioned, this issue went on for years before it was resolved. She shared that this situation took a toll on her physical health and energy levels. She saw the incident as wrong, but regarded it as just something that black women typically deal with. With limited education and the need for healthcare benefits, Delilah sustained her composure until the rough times passed.

Shantay, a student at a predominantly white institution, provided an example that made her experiences in the dorm extremely stressful and unpleasant. According to Shantay, there was only one other African American student, a male, living in her dorm hall. The two of them often found themselves targets of racist jokes. Shantay commented,

> I've lived now on campus for two years and I lived in a dorm with quite a few different ethnicities of people. My roommate was Chinese, the girl across the hall from me was Asian and some Hispanics were upstairs, so there were lots of different cultures. And yet when I moved in I was the only African American person in the dorm in that hall, and so when I was trying to hang out with all of the people in the dorm because they would have barbecues and stuff, they have this guy who they referred to as Token. I thought this was just his nickname, but then I realized that he was called Token because he was their token black guy, and then when I came around, I kind of messed up his nickname a little bit because he was no longer the only black person in the dorm. And so when someone was explaining that to me, I was just like, wow, so next they'll try to think of a nickname for me. And that's just what happened. Their nickname for me ended up being Shout-Out, and it's because they felt that black

people, whenever they got on the radio, they're always getting or giving shout-outs. When I questioned them about it, they claimed that it was easier to pronounce Shout-Out instead of Shantay. So, I was Shout-Out and he was Token. I really didn't want to start any arguments with anybody, so I didn't say much. The white students would crack these racist jokes. I was thinking, okay that's fine because that's the relationship that he [Token] has with them, but then he left and they started cracking the jokes with me and I was like, "Hey, you don't know me like that. I'm not comfortable with that," and so I had to deal with, like, a lot of racism and racist jokes from the white people within my dorm.

We see in Shantay's example that she had to deal with the stressors invoked by white students as a direct result of her race. Even more striking is that Shantay experienced similar bouts of discrimination throughout the campus environment. Although she did not report any of the incidents to campus administrators, she admitted that these conditions caused considerable amounts of stress and that venting to friends and family was the only strategy she employed to alleviate her stress.

The women's accounts mirror what Jones and Shorter-Gooden refer to as "shifting." They argue that the existing oppressive conditions in US society cause black women to shift in order to adjust for differences in race, gender, and class. Thus, there appears to be a disconnect between what one is and what one pretends to be. The authors provide a description of this phenomenon:

> Shifting is what she does when she speaks one way in the office, another way to her girlfriends, and still another way to her elderly relatives. It is what may be going on when she enters the beauty parlor with dreadlocks and leaves with straightened hair, or when she tries on five outfits every morning looking for the best camouflage for [her] ample derriere.[22]

Over time, shifting has devastating effects on the black woman's sense of self. This often includes instances of verbally silencing herself and suffering from depression. Playing multiple roles is exhausting and extremely stressful, and has physical and psychological effects on the individual.

Contrary to what we might think, success does not immunize black women against discrimination. In fact, Joe Feagin and Melvin Sikes interviewed one very successful black entrepreneur who describes her experiences as a black woman as "psychological warfare." Thus, what we begin to see here is that racism and oppression have real consequences. We are finding that long-term periods of exposure to racism can have debilitating psychological effects on people of color and even more so on women of color.[23]

### Unrealistic Expectations Placed on Black Women

Black women spoke directly about the prejudice and discrimination that they regularly encounter in supposedly professional settings. Yet many participants affirmed that racial and gender stereotypes extend beyond the professional setting and they argue that there are widespread consequences to occupying subordinate racial and gender statuses in the United States. A combination of gender and racial statuses leads to a unique set of challenges for black women. Interviewee Alison spoke of the stress she undergoes just living day to day:

> Being the only black female in wherever you work or in whatever class you're taking is exhausting. Not to mention, at the same time, having to live up to the expectations that society in general has for a black female as a wife or a mother.

We see here that Alison's awareness of external expectations weighs heavy on her mind. I later asked her to speak to the extent of stress that these expectations can cause, and she said, "It creates extra stress because you have to do more than what is necessary or required. This wouldn't be stressful if you had to do this for a day or so, but throughout our entire lives! This is too much."

Ava, a married woman, said the unrealistic expectations placed on black women remain a primary stressor for black women in this day and age. With that said, Ava's response to these expectations seems likely to perpetuate this stress. She revealed,

> For years, we've always been told, "you've got to be the best, you've got to be better than everyone else." Unfortunately, the reward for black women in this society is marginal. So you're never going to be

rewarded the same for the amount of effort you're putting in. We have to be three times as good, and so you often walk away from situations feeling disappointed.

The disappointment that Ava spoke of has greatly influenced her viewpoint on living as a black woman. From her standpoint, black women should do their best to live up to expectations in order to minimize stress and disappointment. She stated, "I think we should be strong and to be able to do it all . . . and so I'm right there trying to do it all."

Similarly, study participant Karen argued that just being an African American woman in the United States generates stress:

> Being black in itself is stressful because . . . you're still not viewed as equal to your white or male counterparts. Even though we've got a black president, you still, a lot of times, are not looked on as equal.

Despite the fact that studies show the majority of white Americans believe we live in a postracial society,[24] Karen's point calls attention to the difficulty of being black and female today. When asked to describe how she deals with this dilemma, Karen acknowledged that she has yet to find an effective way to change the situation and admitted that she deals with it the best way she knows how: "I just try to express it to anyone that will listen, but if you see there's no change, then you just try to find another job or whatever else you need to keep your sanity. Eventually something will give."

Similarly, Cheryl spoke about the stressors that come along with black women's attempts to navigate prevalent racist and gendered assumptions:

> I think white people take black women for granted. They have assumptions about us and they see us in a different light. So I think the whole Ralph Ellison thing about the "invisible man," there is that sense of invisibility about us. They really don't respect us and they really don't see us as equals. That perception places a bit of a hardship on blacks. It's very subtle and it does affect our performance in life, and to some extent it affects what we do in life. Sometimes we struggle trying to figure out how white people see us or what's their reaction going to be to this or that? So I think racism creates a subtle hindrance to our survival in this country.

Cheryl later shared that she deals with these types of stressors through writing. She considers her diary a place to purge, a place where she can reflect on her day and assess its occurrences.

## A Balancing Act

To gain a full understanding of the notion of black womanhood, it is important to first discuss the construction of womanhood in America. The lives of US women during the nineteenth century were significantly influenced by the notion of the "cult of womanhood," which comprised a set of attitudes and beliefs that were fundamental in establishing behavioral expectations for women's home and family lives. Women were held to these stringent guidelines by their husbands, their communities, and, more importantly, by society, with its principles for measuring her womanhood. These imageries were reinforced through media outlets ranging from magazines to religious manuals. And, as one might imagine, there were women who surpassed society's image of what a woman should be, just as there were women who fell short.[25]

Narrow definitions of womanhood proved particularly problematic for black women. Around the same time that notions of "true womanhood" were constructed, a conflicting ideology that applied exclusively to black women also emerged. Images of the mammy, the matriarch, the sapphire, and the jezebel all sought to control black women through the process of othering.[26] Thus, while white women were encouraged to live up to the standards of "true womanhood," black women were encouraged to live up to standards of "deviant womanhood."[27]

US women have generally endured gender stereotypes. While white women have had to contend with assumptions about their passivity and weakness, African American women have had to challenge myths surrounding the strong black woman. Shaida Muhammad's article in *Ebony* magazine emphasized some of the real-life consequences of myths of the strong black woman. For instance, she states, "I have seen many women in my life literally become ill from taking on everyone's problems; counseling family and friends, working multiple jobs, taking in children, housing relatives—essentially catering to everyone else's needs but their own."[28]

Muhammad's points were affirmed in a *Washington Post* survey that suggested black women were more likely than whites (men and women) to have loaned money to a friend or family member, helped a friend or family member with childcare, or helped an elderly friend or family member on a regular basis.[29]

Along these lines, more than half of the black women in my study acknowledged that their busy schedules leave little time for self-care. A noteworthy finding of this study was black women's awareness of their overburdened responsibilities (commonly to their friends, family, and community) as a stressor. Black women recognize the value that they bring to their families, communities, and social circles, yet they often overextend themselves. My discussion with Alisha speaks directly to the point of black women putting the needs of others before their own. Alisha has one daughter and two sons, and she admitted that she has taught her daughter (but not her sons) the importance of being present for others:

> I think the biggest mistake that African American females make with their female children is that we always tell them that they are supposed to make sure that everything goes right. This is how I was brought up. You are the pillar of the family. This is a message that we hand down to our girls from generation to generation. I tell her all the time, irregardless of what goes on, if something happens to me, your brothers are going to be looking to you. She's not the older but she's the girl.
>
> You know, I don't know why it is that there is a consensus in the black community that the black female is the stronger of the species. But, I just feel like we can take so much more—oh, God dipped down real low when he made the black female. Oh, we can take so much. You know, I think about even in slavery when the [black] woman was taking care of the white woman's house, she has to go down and deal with the white woman and her problems all day long then come home and deal with hers. But she was able to do that and still get up the next day and start all over again.

Alisha admitted that coaching her daughter to devote herself wholeheartedly to others could come with physical and emotional costs. Although she realizes that black women pay a cost, she also believes the role that black women play in their communities is invaluable.

Participants often shared details of their never-ending schedules. Although the majority of the women rely heavily on their families for support of one kind or another, more than half of the women reported that their obligations to family and friends were a significant stressor in their lives. Kelly, a full-time cosmetologist, single mother of three, and primary caregiver for her disabled mother, stated,

> I end up really stressed when I try to handle too many things on my own. I am raising children, three children by myself, and I pick up too many things that I don't need to pick up, like extra chores and things for other people. Either I am serving my clients, I am doing things for my mother, my brother, or the kids. There really is no one else in my family that can do these things, so I never really get a break. It becomes stressful and it puts a lot of weight on me.

Similarly, Tina admitted that the stress stemming from her obligations to others has caused her issues. Tina had a stroke at the age of thirty-five. Although her stroke was caused by a preexisting medical condition, she knows that the stressors of being a single mother and caring for countless others only exaggerated the condition. Here Tina discusses her struggle to find time to take care of herself:

> People want you to come here, people want you to come there, and this isn't like work-related stress, which, I am not even going to go there [chuckles]. But I have all these things that I want to get done. I need to go to the mall, I need to get the car washed, I've got to make sure that the oil is changed. I've got to get things for the kids and my mother. I got to do this, I got to do that. So all of these things are piling up and you're like, "I can't do it all, but I've got to because no one else can do it for me." So something ultimately gets neglected, and it's usually me [sighs].

Kelly's and Tina's accounts reveal an interesting dynamic that very few black women openly discuss. The reality regarding black women's obligations to those they care deeply about is often complex. Their obligations to others function simultaneously as the women's biggest stressors and their biggest stress relievers. Caring for others is a central part of black women's identity. Consequently, they place significant value on their involvement in these tasks. Yet, because the women are accustomed to giving their last (material and nonmaterial) resources to those for whom they feel responsible, they often feel guilty for taking time to care for themselves.

Jennifer also communicated the complexities that go along with being a part of a close-knit family. Here she explains why she believes her family is a source of stress:

> Well, according to society, being the oldest sister, it's like I'm the second mom, house manager, babysitter, chauffer, tutor, mentor [laughs]. Basically whatever role people specialize in and get paid for, I'm doing it for free [laughs] for my family. This is my role as the older sister. This has been expected of me since I was younger. Now that I've gone to the PhD [education] level and I'm, like, the first in my family to do that, like, I'm not sure if they really understand, like, what it takes to survive at this level—to understand how that [PhD-level work] affects my personal schedule and time. What can I really do to still help the family? But it's kind of like, even in my own mind, I still feel like that big sister that has to, you know, be there to help with the homework and take them to basketball practice. So even I myself struggle with, you know, prioritizing my work to my family obligations, partly because I know what my family expects of me.

In Jennifer's example, there is absolutely no question of whether she loves her family, but the stress comes about when Jennifer is unable to follow through on her familial obligations. On the other hand, she expressed that, in part, her devotion to her family persists because she trusts that her family would do the same for her:

> My mom would have no problem taking me back [allowing me to move back] home to Houston. I have so many relatives and friends in Houston. I'm blessed that there will never come a time where I wouldn't have a place to stay or food to eat. This is why I get stressed when my schedule doesn't allow me to help family the way I think I would like.

Black women play key roles in their social circles. Yet it is important to acknowledge that informal support systems may generate an entirely different form of stress for black women.[30]

## *Financial Want*

Black women are disproportionately affected by poverty. Therefore, the issue of "want" or "lack" continually emerged from the women's narratives regarding stressors in their daily lives. Insufficient financial and material resources were constant concerns for several of the women. Cheryl communicated that finances are one of the most significant stressors in her life. She is a single woman with no children and a reported annual income between $15,000 and $29,999. She refuses to let financial troubles discourage her, and she illustrated this point by stating, "I'm living on loans. I'm almost fifty years old. I'm in debt up to my ears and I'm trying to figure out how I'm going to pay all these people off before I die, so that's a big stressor for me. Money—there's never enough money!" Cheryl is employed full-time, but she is also a full-time graduate student. She plans to have her PhD in hand by the time she is fifty-two years old. She acknowledged that obtaining her degree takes financial sacrifice. Nonetheless, she communicated that the stress of trying to make ends meet is difficult.

Katherine reported that she is experiencing severe economic hardship. With an annual income in the $30,000–$49,999 range, Katherine is a single mother of four adult daughters, the youngest being twenty-eight years old. All of her daughters have children of their own, and all are single mothers to those children. Because each of her daughters struggles financially, Katherine feels compelled to support them and her grandchildren as much as she can. She admits that the divide between her desire to help her family and her lack of finances has resulted in stress and anxiety:

> I am really stressed because I'm going through some financial issues right now. I have to definitely find some other type of work . . . and just do whatever I can for my grandkids to become successful. I need to become financially stable so that I can definitely help them out. So far, no, I haven't achieved it [financial success] the way that I would like to, but I've been pretty successful in the past.

Katherine admits that she has suffered from panic attacks and insomnia. The attacks began shortly after her in-home child daycare business slowed down. Katherine and her children rely heavily on her stream of income, so her recent drop in income has created a difficult situation.

Donna and her family have also experienced rough economic times. Donna, married with three children, has a reported annual household income of $30,000–$49,999. Her family's income was recently reduced because her husband was injured in a car accident. She suddenly found herself taking on the role of primary breadwinner for her family. She shares how this is causing her significant stress:

> I work two jobs to make ends meet. It's a stressful thing to not know day to day what is going to happen economically in this society. But I try not to worry about that because in all actuality, I'm not promised tomorrow. So I try not to dwell on that too much.

Donna shared that she typically leaves the house around 7:15 a.m. to drop off the kids at school, arrives at work by 8 a.m. and leaves by 4:30 p.m., then starts her part-time night shift at 5 p.m. and clocks out around 9 p.m. In addition to taking on the financial responsibilities for her family, she reported that her body is starting to feel the physical effects of these long hours. What is noteworthy about her story is that despite getting little relaxation time, Donna reports consciously taking time to uplift her husband. She professes, "There is no 'I'm the head of the household because I work two jobs.' . . . No matter what, he still makes the last decision."

We repeatedly see in these accounts that incidents of prejudice and discrimination, familial obligations, and financial lack serve as primary stressors in the lives of African American women. In fact, these narratives reveal that black women may suffer from multiple stressors. So then the question becomes, *What effects are these stressors having in the lives of black women?*

## I Just Want the Pain to End

Since suicide is unlikely to occur among African American women, their accounts are largely missing from the research. Thoughts of ending it all speak to the varying experiences among participants, some of whom, at the very least, considered suicide. Although black women's suicide-completion rate is significantly lower than the rates of all other groups, their suicide-attempt rate is roughly the same as white women's.[31] Just over one-third of the thirty-three interviewees in my study had at least briefly considered suicide at some point in their lives. Of the women who confessed to considering suicide, four classified their thoughts as "casual," five classified their thoughts as "serious," and two divulged that their thoughts led to an actual attempt.

This section summarizes the reoccurring themes that emerged in response to the question "Have you ever considered suicide?" For the women who responded yes, I further examined the circumstances under which they considered suicide. One might assume that the unremitting stressors of black women discussed earlier in this chapter would increase the probability of attempts and/or completion rates. Nonetheless, my study concludes that these factors rarely resulted in suicidal behavior. In most cases, the women conveyed that they just wanted the "pain" of their current situation to end. In sharing their scenarios of "wanting the pain to end," two subthemes emerged from the women's accounts; I refer to the first subtheme as casual thoughts and the second subtheme as ideations. Let's first examine participants' assessments of these thoughts.

## *Casual Thoughts*

Many of the women described their thoughts as not uncommon, considering their circumstances. They conveyed that based on the large amounts of stress that they were under, most in their shoes would likely think of suicide at least once. In most cases, once they worked through the situation, thoughts of suicide dissipated. Although several women expressed that they had considered suicide at one time or another, those who communicated this as a casual thought followed up by stating that taking their own life was not an option.

In reply to the question "Have you ever considered suicide?" Janet stated, "Yes, I thought about it but, uh, it's not an option for me. I don't know if it was really ever an option or that I really thought about actually doing it." For Janet, a divorced woman, the thoughts surfaced during an extremely stressful time. She explains, "I think that everyone thinks about suicide from time to time, so I didn't take it too serious."

She ultimately credits her belief in God as her primary reason for not following through.

Tanya, a single woman, also expressed her experiences with contemplating suicide in an informal way. When asked "Have you ever considered suicide?" she stated,

> Not seriously, I mean, there are thoughts when you're definitely like, things might be better if I weren't existing, but I have never got to the point where I thought about, here's what I'm going to do, and this is how I'm going to do it.

She later shared that two of her cousins committed suicide and seeing the ravaging impact that the events had on her family made it even less likely that she would take her own life. Furthermore, although Tanya's thoughts of suicide were genuine, like Janet, she considered them to be a common response to stressful situations. Tanya credited her Christianity for her not following through on these thoughts.

Tina, a single woman, also reported a time when she considered suicide:

> In my opinion, everybody thinks of suicide in low stages or just through life. It's like, I just want this to stop, how I wish I would die—you know. Looking back, there's no way I could have taken my own life. There's no way to learn anything from what you are going through; your life would be over.

Although Tina was going through a rough time in her life, she believed that these thoughts were harmless:

> I mean, I can't imagine actually killing myself. Thinking about it and actually doing something to make it happen were two different things for me. I mean, we quickly say, "I want to die" because we want something to end, but to actually take the action, I never came close to doing that.

Tina said that her commitment to her family was her primary reason for not following through with the act. She later declared that nothing could happen that could push her to carry out the act.

These narratives reveal that thoughts of suicide were not perceived to be serious. In fact, some of the women considered occasional thoughts of suicide to be normal. Lastly, of the women who experienced casual thoughts, none of them shared those thoughts with others. Preliminary study data suggest that this may have been due to the fact that they had no intent to harm themselves and they realized that their levels of stress were significantly elevated.

## Ideations

The Centers for Disease Control and Prevention (CDC) defines a suicide attempt as a nonfatal, self-directed, potentially injurious behavior with an intent to die as a result of the behavior. A suicide attempt may or may not result in injury. Additionally, the CDC defines suicidal ideations as thinking about, considering, or planning for suicide.[32]

While some study participants' thoughts of suicide were unlikely to develop into action, as we saw in the previous section, other women revealed that their thoughts of suicide were preliminary steps to the act itself. Different from those who spoke of casual thoughts of suicide, these women revealed that they perceived their thoughts to be genuine. In other words, they claimed that these were not mere thoughts, and they did not perceive them as normal and knew that they should seek outside help. For example, Delilah contemplated suicide after the sudden loss of her husband. When asked "Have you ever considered suicide?" Delilah stated,

> Very slightly, and when I say that, I lost my husband five years ago. There was a moment that I knew I was in trouble when I just thought that life wasn't the same, wasn't as I had known it, so I knew I needed to reach out. But I got help, and I took antidepressants for a while; I guess about three months. My doctors said I probably should have stayed on them longer. But I think the meds got me through that point where I just felt lost.
>
> I continued to work and go out with friends and everything. I did share with one of my coworkers how I felt, and that was the only person that I told that sometimes I just don't think I want to go on, but I knew suicide wasn't an option. But that is the only time that I had ever seriously thought of it [suicide], but I knew I couldn't do it.

After I probed a bit further to gain insight into what altered her suicidal thoughts, Delilah shared that her not attempting suicide was due to religious beliefs. She lives by the religious principles instilled in her at a very young age, which taught her that suicide is just not an option.

Tasha, a married woman, also seriously considered ending her life. During a difficult time in her life, as a teenager, Tasha saw suicide as a way out of a dreadful situation. A combination of a difficult upbringing and the lack of control over the situation resulted in thoughts of ending her life:

> As a child, there were times when I wanted to end some of the issues that I was facing. I grew up in a blended family that had a lot of problems. And so as a child you do not really see your options, you do not really have control and you do not have the emotional maturity to handle the situation, so you may think drastic things, not really realizing what that would really mean, not really fully understanding.

Tasha said that she has matured a great deal since then and would no longer consider suicide an option. She revealed that commitment to her family and friends in addition to her spiritual growth helped strengthen her during this complicated time.

Shantay attempted to end her life during the summer of her eighth-grade year. During this time, she experienced very difficult conditions for a fourteen-year-old girl. Upon losing her mother, she decided life wasn't worth living anymore:

> I was just feeling really bad at one point in time and in transition really from middle school to high school and that was around the time when my mom passed away, after I graduated from the eighth grade. And so when I was getting ready to go into high school, everyone [kids at school] was talking about the things they were doing with their mom, and their mom bought them all of this and everything. And I know Gran [grandmother] said my mother didn't raise me, but she was there and then I guess just dealing with her death and being a new student in my high school and everything, it was just, I don't know. It was really intense, and my older sister—she's ten years older than me, so she wasn't around at that time when I was starting school. I mean, she bought me some clothes and sent them to me, but nothing more than that. And so I guess at one point in

time I was just feeling really down emotionally, and I started to consider suicide. Oh, and I think also at that time, because if I remember correctly, my grandfather passed away the year before my mom passed away. So I didn't even have that father figure in my life anymore, so it was just me and my grandma when I was starting school.

Shantay shared her thoughts of suicide with her grandmother, who supported Shantay through this ordeal. Similar to Tasha, Shantay said she has matured a great deal since those days. She credits the support of her family and social networks for helping her through this dark time.

## Summary

We repeatedly see that black women face multiple stressors in their lives. A closer look at black women's lives reveals disproportionate rates of poverty and depression and stressors within their families, all alongside living within a racist, sexist society.

Logically the question becomes, If black women's lives are significantly more challenging than other Americans' and they do at least entertain thoughts of suicide, then why do their rates of suicide remain virtually nonexistent? We see here that thoughts of suicide do not materialize into behavior in most cases. Therefore, black women's suicide rate defies nearly all of the existing literature on suicide, particularly as it relates to suicide risk factors. Given that, social scientists find black women's suicide rates intriguing. As I established in Chapter 1, this study is dedicated to exploring the paradoxical relationship between black women's suicide rates and their unique social position. The next three chapters provide insight into black women's self-proclaimed safeguards against suicidal behavior and provide detailed illustrations of black women's reasons for not committing the act.

In Chapter 3 I discuss the ways in which religion and faith-based beliefs influence black women's perceptions of suicide. Dating back to slavery, faith and religion have been cornerstones of the black community. Black women admit that life's challenges can be unrelenting; however, their faith provides a noteworthy approach to dealing with contemporary difficulties.

Black women believe that their religious affiliations and/or beliefs, like their social networks, are central to the way they view acts of suicide. The notion of faith-based beliefs unravels yet another component of the puzzling suicide paradox.

## Chapter 3
## I Give All the Glory
### The Role of Faith in Black Women's Perceptions of Suicide

> *I think we look at people as crazy [laughs] that commit suicide. And I think a lot of it has to do with religion because we consider this [body] as God's temple. You know, and whether it's Baptist or Methodist, Catholic, whichever, we were raised that this is God's temple and you don't destroy God's temple. I think we [blacks] have a major issue with that.*
>
> —Kyndall[1]

Vivian Green, an R&B artist, seriously contemplated suicide shortly after the birth of her son, Jordan. When Jordan was a newborn, doctors diagnosed him with a mysterious rare illness. He was not expected to live a week. Doctors warned Green that if Jordan did survive, he would be mentally challenged. This grim prognosis coupled with a recent breakup sent Green into an emotional tailspin. She recalls, "I definitely didn't want to be here. I didn't think it could get any lower than that."

Green credits her faith for saving her life. She states that her faith grew exponentially during those times. Her belief that God is in control helped her to refocus her energy on the reasons why God chose her to parent this child. She began to see this challenge as a blessing: "My spiritual growth skyrocketed. Sometimes you have no choice but to believe God knows what He's doing. I realized that He chose me to be this child's mother, so He thinks I'm strong enough to handle it." Jordan is now a healthy eight-year-old. He continues to develop at a healthy rate, and has surpassed doctors' expectations.[2]

Green's story reaffirms existing literature indicating that faith-based beliefs and religious affiliation appear to have some preventive effect on suicide behavior, particularly among African American women.[3] The literature also suggests that being involved in a religious group, partaking in church activities, and belonging to close-knit communities promote social integration.[4] This is particularly important because religiosity is associated with better psychological health as well as a decrease in suicidal ideation among African Americans.[5]

Studies suggest that church attendance has an influence on ethnic differences in suicide acceptability.[6] For example, research has uncovered a positive association between lower suicide rates and religion and spirituality among African American women.[7] Kevin Early conducted an ethnographic study that examined the effects of the black church on suicide. The accounts presented in his study highlight widespread attitudes and beliefs against suicide in the black church. He also found that church attendance played a critical role in the African American perception of suicide as a "white thing."[8] He concluded that antisuicidal beliefs contribute to the low level of suicide acceptability in the black community.

In this chapter I show that religion and/or faith-based beliefs are at the forefront of discussions of factors that most likely buffer the risk of suicidal behavior among black women. Thus, it was no surprise that well over three-fourths of the women in my study considered themselves to be active members of a church or religious group. The findings suggest that religion and faith-based beliefs are critical in constructing black women's negative perceptions of suicide. In fact, twenty-nine of the thirty-three women in this study directly mentioned religion as fundamental to their perceptions of the suicide paradox. The collection of narratives in this chapter transcend the surface conversations to reveal something much deeper than black women's faith-based perspectives; these firsthand accounts offer insight into how such beliefs activate a set of principles on which black women rely to develop their perceptions of suicide. The narratives reveal the practical ways in which these beliefs safeguard against a decision to end one's life.

An essential distinction worthy of highlighting early in this discussion is that most of the time the terms *religion, faith,* and *spirituality* were used interchangeably in the participants' narratives. When asked to clarify what they meant by *religious beliefs*, all but four respondents elucidated the term with another one: *Christianity*. Though social connectedness inevitably plays a critical role in black women's religious experience, this study's findings reveal more deeply how faith-based beliefs materialize into life-guiding principles that ultimately avert suicidal behavior.

By no means should the women's narratives be taken to diminish the importance of social connectedness within the religious group experience. Throughout this study black women commonly cited their faith-based beliefs and their personal relationship with their higher power (most commonly the Christian God) as a separate and almost superseding layer of protection against suicidal ideations and other life challenges. The women often commented that even when they were alone, they had Jesus. Their notions of faith, around which their personal decisions to avoid suicide orbited, seemed especially to entail their respective perceptions of a higher power. In fact, because of the complexity and pervasiveness of these discussions of a personal relationship with a higher power, these findings are presented separately from the role religion plays in promoting social integration in lieu of suicide. Within the context of faith-based beliefs as they relate to the racial suicide paradox, these women ultimately referenced their decision to one day face the judgment of their God rather than the judgment of their religious social groups or family members.

## Black Women's Religious Practices

According to the 2008 US Religious Landscape Survey, black women disproportionately constitute the largest group of Christians.[9] Blacks are noticeably more religious in myriad measures compared to the rest of the US population. Measures ranging from religious affiliation to attendance at religious services, frequency of prayer, and religion's general significance prove consistently higher for African Americans. Thus, not surprisingly, barely 1 percent of African Americans classify themselves as atheist or agnostic.[10] Additionally, a 2011 poll taken by the *Washington Post/*Kaiser Family Foundation revealed that 74 percent of black women in the United States considered living a religious life to be very important, compared to 70 percent of black men, 57 percent of white women, and 57 percent of white men. The poll also found that an astonishing 87 percent of black women believed the role of religion or faith in God was very important in helping them get through tough times, compared to 66 percent of white women, 79 percent of black men, and 51 percent of white men.[11] Analogously, Rheeda Walker, David Lester, and Sean Joe reported that African Americans were more likely to believe that the quality of their lives and their general well-being were attributable to God, whereas whites were more likely to believe that an individual or a governmental influence was responsible for the quality of their lives and well-being.[12]

For African American women, employing religion as a means to navigate stressful situations is not a new concept.[13] Although Kumea Shorter-Gooden did not specifically attribute religious upbringing as a preventive measure against suicide, she did contend that black women often rely on their beliefs in a higher power to persevere. It is no coincidence that nearly 90 percent of black women in the United States believe religion to be very important in helping them get through tough times, compared to 60 percent of white women. The question thus becomes, *What has occurred in the lives of black women that encourage them to turn to a higher power during troubling times?*

Corresponding to the general US population, religion and faith-based beliefs proved vital in the lives of the interviewees in this study. Their narratives revealed a stimulating take on the ways in which faith and religious affiliations discourage suicidal behavior. The interviewees offered rather expansive insight into the roles that these beliefs play in relation to the suicide paradox in black women's lives.

## How Black Women's Religious Beliefs Influence Suicide

### *Raised to Put God First*

Early in this study, I prioritized the investigation of why black women deem religion significant in their lives. African American women often credit their upbringing as the source of their beliefs, and this factor significantly relates to how religion and its relationship to suicide function in their lives. In direct reference to black women's explanations for their low suicide rate, more than half of the respondents identified religion or faith-based beliefs as one of the top three reasons for black women's low rate of suicide. Interestingly, the stories of non-Christian study participants revealed that most of them were raised under Christian principles. Thus, their perspectives on the topic of suicide were virtually indistinguishable from those of the Christian respondents. Both groups of women used the terms *faith, spirituality,* and *religion* interchangeably.

In numerous accounts, women in the study discussed how deeply ingrained their religious and spiritual beliefs are. In fact, they often explained that early in their childhood they were socialized to turn to the spiritual realm during troubling times. Furthermore, they asserted that they most commonly learned how and when to turn to God from close friends and family members. For example, Tasha recalled learning how to deal with life's stresses from her family:

> I recall watching my grandmother and my uncle when I was a child. She [grandmother] was a very, very strong Christian. She dealt with stress through prayer. When times were good and when times were bad, she would pray. My uncle was quite a unique man. Very different. He was a man of quiet strength. But he really did, I think, model Christ's example in his life in the way he treated people. So he was a quiet strength where he said what needed to be said. He did not yell it. He just said it and then he did whatever he needed to do. I think I model more after my uncle. When I am calm, I can think about it [the problem], and I think, okay, this is a better way. When I get beyond reason, that is when I pray.

Tasha's childhood memories focused on her grandmother's and her uncle's responses to life challenges and the fact that she modeled her responses to stress in a similar manner. She admired the source of her uncle's "quiet strength." She recognized early on that belief in Jesus Christ resulted in insurmountable strength. Moreover, with that strength she realized that she could handle life's smallest and greatest challenges.

Respondent Tanya shared that as a child she closely watched her father's responses to stress. Although Tanya self-identified as a Christian, she stated,

> My dad had more of a temper, so he was a little bit more explosive when he was upset or something. But he also, at other times, was very meditative. He was a Muslim so he would read the Quran and meditate on the scriptures to try to relieve some of the stress.

Although many of the participants recognized that their family members used spiritual tactics to handle stress, they most commonly stated that the origin of these practices was beyond their recollection. They believed that their family members most likely learned these techniques from their parents and passed them down from generation to generation.

Sandy's grandmother was instrumental in her upbringing. Although her mother was her primary caregiver, as a young child Sandy spent much time observing her grandmother's approach to handling life's difficulties:

> Well, growing up, I can't remember my grandmother being stressed too much. She always just kind of kept herself busy. And she was definitely a religious person and very close to God. She spent a lot of time praying and reading her Bible. She always just kind of knew that God would fix it. She rubbed off on me because sometimes I'll get to the point with stress where I kind of keep things to myself, that I don't want to talk about it too much. But somehow, just like my grandmother, I just know that God will fix it.

Sandy disclosed that she was not an active member of a church or religious organization and rarely attended a formal church service, but she rated her relationship with God as "pretty good." She believed that participation in the formal sense was far less important than having a close and intimate relationship with her God. She also made it a point to ensure that her teenage daughter spent time with Sandy's mother and grandmother so that they could supplement the faith-based teachings and practices that Sandy herself did not provide.

Kelly, a cosmetologist and self-identified Christian, spoke of the invaluable lessons that she learned as a child from her godmother. Kelly said that "she just *prayed* about it." When I asked her to elaborate what she meant by *it*, she affirmed that "*it* means *everything*." Kelly, who at the time of this study had four children of her own, explained,

> My godmother taught me so much when it comes to dealing with stress. Just like her I now pray, and I wait on God. I am teaching my children to do the same. Black women are heavy religious believers. Deep down inside, they've been rooted in something and they know they cannot do that [suicide] to themselves.

Karen's and Bridgett's accounts revealed that they also perceived religious upbringing as a major factor in minimizing the likelihood that black women will participate in suicidal behavior. Karen, a self-identified Christian and an active member of her local church group, attributed her adamant perspective about suicide to her religious upbringing and personal beliefs about God. She explained, "I was taught that God forgives us for everything, but he don't forgive you for suicide, so I never wanted to venture going to hell." Karen stated that she had never contemplated suicide and credited attending church and believing in God for this resolve, and that her religious upbringing made it difficult for her to see life from any other perspective. She also shared that prayer was her overall solution for dealing with life's difficult events.

Bridgett, a single, childless woman, provided a similar example of how a religious upbringing helped her maintain her antisuicide perspective. Like Karen, she affirmed that a religious upbringing plays a significant role in the low suicide rate of black women:

> I believe that our religious background is a deterrent to committing suicide, and the other thing is, I don't really know the statistics offhand, but a lot of African American women grow up in the church, even more so than black men. You know, every time I go to church, I see a majority of women, and so if that's the case, and if some of it is connected to their religious teachings, then that could be another reason why black women may not commit suicide as much, because they may have more connection to some religious teachings throughout the course of their lives. It has certainly shaped how I see the act.

Bridgett, also an active member of a church group, considered the messages gained through her religious upbringing as critical to her perspective on suicide. Based on Bridgett's account, religious upbringing and current connections to the church seem to be fundamental in deterring black women from suicide.

An interesting finding emerged among the non-Christian and atheist participants in the study. Even though Nina, Robin, Kyla, Terri, and Clara self-identify as Muslim, Buddhist, or atheist, most of them were raised around primarily Christian principles. Therefore, as previously mentioned, their viewpoints about suicide were nearly indistinguishable from those of Christian study participants. For example, despite the fact that Kyla is now a practicing Buddhist, her family still encourages her to partake in Christian traditions, and she often obliges. Her take on this obviously complicated issue is as follows:

> Even if you're not Christian—like I'm not—I know how important the black church is. It's more of an extension of our family, and I even feel that now, like I'm very connected with my grandmother's church, because all of my relatives have gone there and that's the only church she's [her grandmother] known. It is definitely an extension of the black family, and we don't promote suicide in that arena. Regardless of what your religious affiliation is, I think that the black church in America has such a strong connection to the black family, regardless of what you believe in.

Clara, a self-proclaimed atheist, found herself in a similar dilemma to Kyla's. Her beliefs conflicted with her family's Catholic principles. Clara grew up in an upper-middle-class community and her mother died when she was just five years old. A maternal aunt, uncle, and a host of extended family members raised her. She admitted that remnants of her Catholic upbringing remained:

> I am very much the result of how I was raised and how I was socialized within the Catholic Church. I was raised to believe that suicide is considered an absolute no-no. There is an overwhelming commitment of African Americans, and in particular African American women, to religion, Christianity. In fact, if you kill yourself you're out of luck all the way around, okay? So I think among Catholics it is particularly rare. I think one of the things that really crossed my mind was, you know, my mother died when I was five, okay? And even though I'm an atheist, it's

been sort of a silent prayer of mine, particularly as I'm a single mother, don't let me die until he's [her son] safely on his own.

Despite her personal beliefs about religion, she made a decision to baptize her only son in order to ease her family's concerns about where his soul would spend eternity. Even though Clara is an atheist, she loves her family and respects their belief in a higher power.

In summary, the vast majority of the study's participants believed that they internalized the spiritual messages passed from family members during the early years of their lives. Black women's religious upbringing and strong faith-based beliefs appear to play roles in shaping their perspectives on the notion of suicide. Studies have found that black women who attend church regularly tend to be much less tolerant of suicidal ideations than those who do not. These findings suggest that church attendance contributes to existing ethnic differences in suicide acceptability, while encouraging social integration.[14] However, this study found that perceptions of the notion of suicide remained consistent regardless of the level of activity in a formal religious organization. The religious messages passed on to black children, particularly black female children, seem to remain instrumental in their lives, no matter their level of religious commitment later in life.

## A Sinful Act

Now that we have established that religious/spiritual messages are deeply rooted in black women's upbringing, the question becomes, *Does holding steadfast to these beliefs influence African American women's perspectives surrounding the act of suicide, and if so, how?* When asked directly about their perspective on African American women's low suicide rate, half of participants conveyed that the act of suicide would displease God.

Continued discussions of black women's low suicide rate revealed that the study participants' ingrained spirituality triggered intense internal convictions about suicide. They considered the act sinful. The interviewees bluntly disclosed that the thought of spending eternity in hell was enough to deter most black women from participating in suicidal behavior.

Tasha found herself contemplating suicide during her teenage years. She had a rough upbringing, and her lack of control over her life caused thoughts of suicide:

> I knew enough to know that suicide was a sin, and so despite the pain that I felt I was like, "Yeah, but suicide is a sin and it is against God," and so my idea of what I would face on the other side would be worse than living. Having the faith and the fact that it's not just looking at what this life has to offer, you know, that there is something better [references to the afterlife]. And what God commands us to do is to fight this fight with His help.

Tasha went on to share that suicide was no longer an option for her, as she had matured mentally and spiritually since the time she considered it.

Tanya also shared how not having time to repent for the sin of suicide, thereby qualifying her to spend eternity in hell, prevented her from attempting suicide during a rough time in her life when she was involved in an abusive relationship and dealing with the difficulties of single motherhood:

> Well, it's my faith because within Christianity and especially within my church, you're taught that killing oneself is condemning yourself to damnation, basically. There is no way to come back unless within that last breath you can completely confess all your sins and everything else. There is no guarantee that you're going to have time to do that. So I think it's the thought of possibly spending eternity in hell because I decided to kill myself that stops most black women. And I think that that's not worth it.

My discussions with Kyndall echoed Tanya's reservations about the moral judgments that suicide brings. Kyndall revealed,

> I was raised Catholic, so it was definitely instilled in me that suicide is wrong. You don't go to heaven if you kill yourself. You absolutely don't go to heaven if you commit suicide. And my friends and I, we don't even discuss it. I don't think our religious beliefs say that suicide is noble. I think that both our cultural and religious beliefs discourage suicide and support self-preservation.

Although Tanya conveyed that she regularly participated as an active member of a church or religious group, while Kyndall did not, both women were certain that God would be displeased with a suicidal act.

Hilldreth also found herself contemplating suicide as a teenager. She was in a serious relationship that she thought would last forever, but it suddenly ended, leading to her suicidal thoughts. However, her apprehensions about hell were enough to impede her pursuit of the act:

> It's our faith in God. Because if we have faith and we believe that things are going to get better. And also, I would say, it's probably because many of us were taught that you commit suicide, then you're going to go to hell, so people think, "Okay, well, I don't want to go to hell, so I'm not going to kill myself," and I know many people that believe that concept.

Hilldreth went on to say that she would no longer consider suicide because she had come to the conclusion that it doesn't solve anything. Although Hilldreth was not an active member of a church or a religious group, she was clear that her discontent with suicide was not out of fear of God's wrath but rather her desire to remain obedient to God by following His word in accordance with biblical scriptures.

Delilah's account revealed that she was also aware of God's discontent with self-harm. She believed that suicide is simply a "no-no" among black women:

> Most of the times, the comment is, we [black women] don't do that [commit suicide]. We don't think about taking our own lives, and that is just not something that is common. We think that that's a no-no. And I think spiritually, we're taught that it's a sin. That is what kind of stays in your head because we were told that you're forgiven for everything but self-murder, which is suicide. So I think that could be one of the things that we kind of hold on to. You don't want to do that. If you take your own life, you're doomed.

The comments revealed thus far in this chapter show a clear connection between the women's accounts and Kyndall's quote at the chapter's opening. Interestingly, her mention of God's temple directly correlates with 1 Corinthians 3:17 (King James version), which states, "If any defile the temple of God, him shall God destroy; for the temple of God is holy, which temple ye are." Many of the accounts within this chapter reveal that African American women liken their bodies to a holy temple. One might assume that the thought of spending eternity in hell would discourage the act of suicide by evoking fear. However, it is important to note that the women did not speak of their beliefs as if they were oppressed and avoiding God's wrath by eluding suicide. Instead, the matter-of-fact knowledge they conveyed involved preserving their bodies and their lives to remain obedient to their higher power.

### Seeking God's Will

*It is not about you—it's about what God is going to do in your life!*
—Bishop T. D. Jakes[15]

Notions of seeking God's purpose for their lives proved to be particularly significant in shaping the women's perspectives regarding stressful events and particularly concerning the women's perspectives on suicide. The narratives illustrate that self-harm and seeking life's purpose are contradictory. In other words, rather than end their lives, these women sought to find God's plan for their lives. Focusing on the intentions of this higher power distracted them from the immediate problem.

Participants admitted that the journey was not always easy, but the path of least resistance involved relinquishing physical and spiritual self-control. The study revealed that the women believed allowing God to take control was accompanied by the promise of protection and guidance. So, then, how does a woman's desire to find her life's purpose affect suicide? In response to the question "Have you ever considered suicide?" Jennifer boldly stated,

> Oh, no, I feel that every day that I have a chance to be on this earth has a purpose, so once I found the Lord, I really . . . it's the motivation that I have every day and also, like, the people who are very close to me in my life, remind me that, you know, all that we've been through is for a reason, so that every day that I have on this earth is, you know, still speaking of that reason why I'm supposed to be here and trying to do the Lord's will.

Jennifer then referenced two biblical scriptures that she believed saved her life:

> I will have to say there's two quotes from two scriptures that I follow, and the one would be that all things good and bad work towards, you know, those who seek the Lord, and basically understanding that all that happens to me is for a reason. His will is for me to fulfill a higher purpose in my life. The second one would be Job 1:21, and it says, "The Lord giveth and the Lord taketh away. Blessed be the name of the Lord." And basically just understanding that everything on this earth is temporary and that people, things, and situations will come and go, but in all things that we should praise the Lord. He has a higher purpose for us. So understanding why it [people, places, and things] was there for whatever time it was and appreciating that, and then using that to, you know, keep on bettering ourselves.

Interestingly, Jennifer seriously contemplated suicide at one time in her life. However, her faith gave her the inspiration to go on to find her purpose. Jennifer attributed her thoughts of suicide to a combination of school, personal issues, and not knowing who she was. Her response to the whole incident was, "It took me finding the Lord. . . . It saved my life." Jennifer revealed that she had become an active member of her church and prioritized doing God's work. Removing the focus from the self and concentrating on fulfilling God's purpose for her life prompted Jennifer to handle stress accordingly. Although she made it clear that suicide was no longer an option, she perceived stress to be a necessity in her journey with Christ.

Alisha, a single woman who served as the primary caregiver for a grandchild, claimed that her Christian teachings instilled in her a sense of belonging to something greater than herself. Alisha revealed that suicide was not an option because she believed her life was not hers to take:

> I know that the Christ that I love loves me that much, so He gave His life for me. Why should I decide to limit something that He's given me? I have received a gift, and every morning when I wake up, I may not be as strong as I used to be twenty years ago, but our parents used to always say in their prayers that He gives me a reasonable portion of health and

strength, so that reasonable portion is enough to get me through the day. So, it's as important to me now and it was when I raised my children that we understand that the life we live is not ours. It's not mine by myself. I owe so many other people. And above all, I owe it all to Him.

Alisha spoke of principles that were instilled in her by her parents as a child and that she, in turn, had endeavored to instill in her own children. Intriguing, too, was Alisha's overall perspective about her life. She was confident in her assertions that God would supply her needs as long as she gave back to God through others. She believed that God's will supersedes her individual notions of self. Therefore, she perceived thoughts of self-harm as simply unreasonable.

Tina and Regina attributed notions of the low suicide rate among black women to their ability to see beyond their individual problems to something greater than themselves. Their life perspectives required them to focus more on God's desires for their lives rather than their own wants. Both women's narratives revealed that seeking God's purpose for their lives resulted in less stress and reduced the likelihood that they would resort to suicidal behavior. Tina stated,

> I take it to God because I've had it. I have to be prayerful and try not to get into a depressed mode. "No, Tina, don't go there." Because I was literally stripped of so much of my independent self, and I believe that was one of the things that God was trying to tell me. You're too independent. Lean on people sometimes. Quit letting yourself stress. Lean on me.

Even though Tina, a single mother, expressed that she was not an active member of a church or religious group, she confirmed that she depended on God for her continued existence in her time of need. Regina, a married woman and an active member of her local church, referenced a time when things seemed fairly grim. Her response to the situation was as follows:

> Pray, pray, pray . . . I pray and praise. I love my praise and worship and I think when I put that on, you forget about the little whatever it is, the dilemma, and you give it to the Lord; and we try to figure things out,

and He's already really worked it out, and if you let go and let Him do it, there ain't no need to worry. We can't do it; we can't fix it. Sometimes we wonder how this is going to happen or how that is going to happen, but he does it all the time. All the time! It's about living in peace, which is the way God wants us to live.

Regina provided additional examples of why she could never consider suicide. She simply put her trust in God to meet her needs:

I don't think I would even consider it, because if I lost my home, I know God would give me a new one. A vehicle—same thing. You know what I'm saying? I don't think I would even . . . I don't think . . . no. Even losing a loved one, because I know . . . and the Lord tells us that we should rejoice when someone is born and . . . I mean rejoice when they leave and be sad when they're born, but we're just the opposite. So no, nothing comes to mind.

It was apparent that God played an invaluable role in Regina's life. I could see emotions begin to surface as she listed the many things that God is capable of resolving. I took a few moments to allow Regina to gain her composure; I then asked her to explain why this was a sensitive issue for her. She conveyed that she had personally seen God fix issues in her life. Because of this, she had learned the importance of seeking God's will for her life. She stated, "People who commit suicide obviously don't have God in their life." She argued that Christians have no need to be stressed, as they have the option to hand their problems directly over to God.

Several of the women conveyed that trying to make things happen by works of their own hand could potentially cause more harm than good and that letting go of selfish desires promotes an antisuicide perspective. They posited that their faith in God positively benefits believers, primarily in two ways. First, the individual no longer focuses on the problem or the need to fix the problem at hand. Second, a pervasive peace emerges when a person operates under the belief that God is guiding his or her steps and that He will not put more on the person than he or she can handle. The women conveyed that tapping into this supernatural power was vitally important to alleviating stress in their lives.

## Let God Bear the Burden

As we saw in Chapter 2, black women's daily stressors are extremely complex. This study revealed that black women have an interesting way of coping with life's challenges. Many of the women in this study learned at an early age to surrender their stressors to God, a practice directly associated with their ability to turn away from the thought of suicide during troubling times. Their narratives offer insight into how their faith-based beliefs detracted from suicidal ideations.

Beyond simply belonging to a religious group, the results showed that religious affiliations and/or faith-based beliefs translated into life-guiding principles that shaped these women's antisuicide convictions. Throughout their interviews, the black women in this study consistently spoke of the importance of allowing God into every aspect of their daily lives. They often became very emotional when citing their religion or faith as a notable reason for their not considering or carrying through with suicide. When this occurred, I probed the respondents and asked them to speak directly about the emotion they experienced, and in nearly every instance the respondents said they experienced joy or gratitude. They greatly appreciated having God on their side, irrespective of the many challenges that they face. Their feelings of gratitude were directly connected to notions of limitless trust in God. They believed that if they trusted and depended on God, He would provide all of their needs. The women admitted that the assumption that they could lean on God offered a sense of liberation that in turn considerably alleviated stress.

The women frequently stated that they had little control over the ultimate outcome of most situations, but they trusted that God was directing them through these situations. In fact, Delilah and Sandy directly cited the serenity prayer as one of the most dominant philosophies in their lives. They mentioned that when life's challenges became unbearable, they recited the prayer. In direct response to why black women's suicide rates stand as they do, Delilah stated,

> One reason for our [black women's] low suicide rate, I think, would be our religious connection. My thought is, and one of my mottos would be the one, the serenity prayer. "God, grant me the serenity to accept

the things I cannot change, the courage to change the things I can, and the wisdom to know the difference." And also knowing that this [the issue at hand] too shall pass.

Delilah proposed that the primary explanation for black women's low suicide rate is religion. Though she has had to personally cope with murder (her cousin, a black female), suicide (her cousin's husband, a white male), and a friend's (black female) near-fatal suicide attempt, she contends that she understands that God is still in control. She has decided to "cast her cares" on him and believes that all will work out in her favor. Sandy's response also speaks to the importance of seeking God's wisdom:

> For me, when it comes to stressful things and certainly the thought of suicide, I very often say it; I don't know if you want to call it like a prayer or a chant, or anything like that. I kind of just say the [serenity] prayer to myself, and I write it down a lot, and I keep it in mind.

Similar to Delilah, Sandy had experienced a tragic murder (her aunt-in-law, a white female) and a suicide (her uncle, a black male). Yet she found her faith in God's control to be comforting. Most interesting about Sandy's and Delilah's accounts is that they both operated under the premise that if something was not working according to their plan, they should surrender it to God.

These accounts merely hint at the ways in which the women believed that God alleviates life's burdens. As Ceva stated, "If God put me in it, God can bring me out." Donna and Karen both believed that suicide is more likely to occur when one gets overwhelmed with the burdens of life. Donna had never personally had suicidal ideations, and she credited this to the overall belief that there was no problem too great for God. She explained:

> I am a very upbeat person, and I go with the flow of life, and I believe in God, you know. He doesn't put more on you than you can bear. You pray about things, and you let them go. You don't try to hold onto things. There are things you can change in life, and there are things that you let play out in life. So you're not . . . you're not taking baggage with you day to day.

Along these same lines, Kelly stated,

> I believe black women deep down inside have a lot more faith, and they really believe things are going to get better. The first reason we don't commit suicide, I still would have to say, would be we have love for God. Suicide, to me, would be for a person that has no way out. I don't think that I would consider that as an option. Under any circumstances. No. You can't bear anybody else's burdens; just deal with your own. Carry your own cross; everybody has their own cross to carry. So if you can pick up somebody else's stuff, then you are superwoman, superman. You just need to carry your own cross—whatever He [God] has placed for you.

Kelly's reference to the cross signifies the crucifixion of Jesus Christ. The Bible teaches Christians that Jesus carried the sins of all humankind to the cross. He was then crucified to wipe away all past, present, and future sins. Therefore, when Kelly said that one must carry one's own cross, she was referring to one's daily problems. She suggested that ultimately each person must tend to his or her own life challenges and must give others room to do the same. She believed that though Jesus can carry the troubles of the world, one person cannot. Kelly's solution was to concentrate on the things that God gives a person to work on, to give others space to deal with their problems, and to cast any burdens onto God.

## Summary

Faith-based or religious beliefs have been established both theoretically and empirically as a factor that decreases the likelihood of suicidal behavior.[16] Émile Durkheim claimed that religion encourages social integration through the formation of collective life. Jan Neeleman, Simon Wessely, and Glyn Lewis discovered that church attendance among African Americans can be correlated with lower levels of suicide acceptability. This chapter offered substantive evidence to support this claim: many of the women expressed that notions of faith-based beliefs significantly shaped their ideas about handling troubling events. Through these narratives, the women exposed how faith-based beliefs permeated their lives on a daily basis.

Much of contemporary suicide literature preserves Durkheim's analysis of religion as significant. Does simply belonging to a religious organization with other devotees discourage suicidal behavior? The literature maintains that being involved in a religious group, partaking in church activities, and belonging to close-knit communities promote social integration. Therefore, religion appears to have a preventive effect on suicide, particularly among African American women. Although previous studies show that religious activities are more likely to safeguard black women against suicidal behavior, they do little to reveal why this is the case. This chapter reveals that focusing only on the role of social integration and faith-based participation in black women's low suicide rates is too simplistic. In fact, this study reveals this notion to be rather reductive.

Black women's narratives within this study reveal an interesting dynamic. Yet again, faith or religion proved significant in developing antisuicide perspectives. The women conveyed that developing a personal relationship with God was most essential in shaping their perspectives about suicide. This often meant that they surrendered to God what they deemed insurmountable obstacles and/or overwhelming circumstances. Their dominant belief was that God is in control. Making it through the trials and tribulations of life for them was less about depending on other human beings than about leaning on and pleasing God. They spoke of God as an ever-seeing and ever-knowing presence. Therefore, even in times when they had no one else, they knew that they could count on God. They could activate their spiritual power by simply calling on their God through faith and prayer.

## CHAPTER 4
## SURVIVAL THROUGH INTERDEPENDENCE
### *FAMILY, COMMUNITY, AND PERCEPTIONS OF SUICIDE*

> *I would say we have low rates of suicide because of our sense of responsibility to others. So much of our experience as a people in this country, our very survival, has really depended upon the female to protect the child during slavery as much as possible, even into somehow maintaining a family, caring for children. I mean, this . . . phenomenon of grandparents, like grandparents taking care of grandchildren, is nothing new for us as a people, not at all. So I would say a sense of responsibility is a strong part of our psyche as a result of our experience as an oppressed group in society. There is overwhelming commitment to other African Americans.*
> —Clare[1]

In reference to black women's low rate of suicide, Clare speaks to the copiousness of black women's responsibilities. Clare was an avid participant in the civil-rights movement and she still considers herself to be a bit of a social activist for equality and justice. In my study she asserted that black women's continual commitment to others protects them from acts of suicide, and that suicide is a selfish act that goes against the psyche of most black women. Clare's comments suggest that black women's oppressive experiences in this country have resulted in high levels of social support. The very survival of African Americans depended on black women forming close-knit bonds with members of their community. In turn, these ties have served as safeguards against suicidal behavior among black women.

The narratives in this chapter illustrate black women's high levels of interdependence within the black community. As a result, nearly two-thirds of the participants stated that their close-knit communities play a significant role in how they perceive suicide. In numerous narratives of black women speaking about their low suicide rate, I discovered that the role of black women as caregivers is central to their self-constructed identities. Their seemingly ever-increasing amount of responsibility leaves them with little time to reflect on their individual challenges. Many of the narratives presented in this chapter reveal that black women's multifaceted networks serve many purposes, and highly interreliant relationships in black women's lives are fundamental to constructing and reinforcing perceptions of suicide as an unacceptable option.

The accounts in this chapter are important because even though it has been suggested that social support systems among African American women are an important protective factor, researchers do not yet fully understand the dynamics of how these support systems operate in relation to the suicide paradox.[2] My data suggest that black women's strong sense of interdependence serves as a protective factor against suicide, and preliminary data seem to suggest that lack of such support may increase their risk. My study confirms the critical importance of African American women's underlying support system in explaining the suicide paradox. Furthermore, my findings reveal not only that social networks are significant in decreasing the likelihood of suicide among African American women, but why.[3]

## The Benefits of Social Networks in the Lives of Black Women

Prior to presenting black women's narratives on the subject, I find it worthwhile to note my conscious decision to separate the discussion of family and social integration (found in this chapter) from the discussion of the key role that religion plays in promoting social integration (covered in the previous chapter). Émile Durkheim argued that religious participation encourages social integration, and I agree. However, I found that the complexity with which black women spoke of their social networks deemed these findings worthy of separation.

We saw in Chapter 3 that black women acknowledged the role of religion as a means of promoting social integration. Faith and religion proved vital in shaping their perceptions of suicide, and commitment to religious principles appears to create internal restraints against suicide. On the other hand, discussions presented in this chapter speak more to black women's external constraints against suicide, which stem from their commitment to others.

Social scientists established the positive benefits of informal social support decades ago. Most of the works contributed to conceptualizing the notion of beneficial social networks in one of three ways. First, earlier studies focused mostly on highlighting the intangible and material aids provided by family members and others outside of an individual's professional networks.[4] Second, more recent studies include the role that social networks play in one's "coping success" amid a variety of groups and life problems.[5] Third, scholars have expanded previous definitions to include an individual's perception that he or she is "loved, valued, able to count on others should the need arise."[6]

Alongside establishing conceptions of social support as material aids, coping success, and individual perceptions, research indicates that social networks influence an individual's psychological well-being.[7] These findings seem to hold true particularly for black women. Paul Nisbet found that black women are less likely than white men and women to seek professional counseling for psychological or emotional troubles and are more likely to rely on friends and family.[8] Years later, Idelle Fraser and her colleagues reaffirmed these findings in their study of African American women coping with domestic abuse.[9] Additionally, strong family cohesion and family support resulted in lower levels of suicidal ideations and depression among black women.[10]

Other scholars have highlighted the importance of black women's interpersonal social ties in relation to their low suicide rate.[11] As noted in Chapter 1, Durkheim's theory of suicide posits that the extent to which one is socially connected impacts his or her likelihood of suicidal behavior. Thus, suicide is most likely to occur in a society characterized with either low or high levels of social integration.[12] Additional research confirms that black women's social networks appear to mitigate their risk of suicide to a greater extent than for any other racial or gender group in the United States.[13]

## Erroneous Claims of Weakening Social Ties in the Black Family

Claims of weakening social networks in the black family are prevalent in the social sciences.[14] In 1965, US Senator Patrick Moynihan claimed, "At the heart of the deterioration of the fabric of Negro society is the deterioration of the Negro family. . . . The white family has achieved a high degree of stability and is maintaining that stability. By contrast, the family structure of lower class Negroes is highly unstable, and in many urban centers is approaching complete breakdown." Moynihan attempted to validate these claims by offering up statistical evidence of disproportionately high female-headed households, divorce rates, and illegitimate births among blacks.

However, despite claims of a "complete breakdown," a closer look at the black family yields a different image.[15] Rather than portraying the black family from a pathological standpoint, more-recent literature acknowledges the strengths of the black family.[16] Robert Hill's review of the literature revealed that a number of traits have proved vital to the black family's survival amid racial oppression in the United States.[17] He suggested traits that include strong kinship bonds; strong work, achievement, and religious orientation; and adaptability of family roles. Allie Kilpatrick suggested that the black family has a unique structure, one that has remained flexible, adaptable, and creative in its endeavors to cope with racist and sexist structural conditions.[18] Therefore, rather than focusing on certain behaviors as pathological, we must acknowledge how these same behaviors have been operative in the survival of the black family.

A closer look at black women reveals their unique social position. Presenting discussions on the historical and contemporary challenges that US black women face is important to understanding this position. Because the primary purpose of this study is to explore black women's perceptions of their extremely low suicide rate despite the disproportionate quantity of stressors in their daily lives, it is critical to have an accurate depiction of the conditions black women encounter on a day-to-day basis. Thus, by merging the suicide literature with the race literature, we may begin to gain insight into how closely suicide risk factors are associated with the daily lives of African American women.

In no way am I attempting to downplay the discrimination and oppression experienced by white women, black men, or any other minority group. However, widespread stereotypical notions of black women often lead to misconstrued perceptions of their realities. Black women are often depicted negatively and viewed as stereotypical mammies, matriarchs, and welfare recipients. Joe Feagin suggests that negative imagery is generally used as a way of expressing antiblack ideas. An example of the overwhelming impact that these images have on society comes from a CBS News/*New York Times* poll, according to which the majority of those questioned, both black and white, thought that most black people were poor and that most welfare recipients were black women. Yet statistics tell us that only 27 percent of blacks are poor compared to 9.9 percent of non-Hispanic whites.[19]

## Black Women's Networks as a Vital Survival Tactic

Both white women and black women continue to be victims of gender oppression in the twenty-first century. However, black women are often criticized for not fitting into traditional sex roles despite the fact that they experience dual discrimination based on both gender and race. Their body parts have been exaggerated, and they are often looked at as hypersexual beings, which can further instigate acts of sexual violence and disrespect toward black women.

Traci West declared that black women's voices are rarely heard, and when they are their opinions are frequently taken out of context. They are considered too emotional or not objective enough. And when it comes to the issue of racism, black women often feel powerless. West interviewed black women in an attempt to grasp how they perceive their position in this country.[20] On the subject of racism, one of the respondents stated,

> Being a black woman is difficult in the United States, to say the least. There's the dictum I would say, in the black community, that men come first. Black men are the ones that are oppressed, and the rest of us need to support them in surviving racism. Like we don't have to survive racism, and we are somehow privileged in this country that we get all the good jobs; we get to go to college and we have it just fine here. And the

poor black men are the ones that we need to somehow reach out to and help, and I don't know, sacrifice our lives for. That has always just struck me as being ridiculous. Anytime at all when racism is discussed in this country, it is discussed in terms of black males. Everyone else is a kind of fodder for their tribulations. That's what I think it means to be a black woman. It's just like this kind of loss of a sense of self. You are just kind of cast away.[21]

Facing multiple forms of discrimination at once is a daily struggle for black women. Unlike for their counterparts (black men and white women), femaleness and blackness are interlocking identities; thus, it is impossible for black women to escape their twofold character. In Aimee Sands's interview with Dr. Evelyn Hammonds, Hammonds presents us with an exceptional example of this point.[22] Concerning her femaleness and blackness, Hammonds states,

They are not separate. Because they are not separate in me. I am always black and female. I can't say, "well, that was just a sexist remark" without wondering would he have made the same sexist remark to a white woman. So does that make it a racist, sexist remark? . . . I don't know. And it takes a lot of energy to be constantly trying to figure out which one it is.[23]

The severity of the oppression that black women have encountered has forced them to reinvent themselves. Over time, black women have discovered that they must play several different roles to survive.

A primary tactic vital to black women's survival has been the use of their social networks. Deborah Gray White, in her book *Ar'n't I a Woman?*, argues that the essentiality of black women's social networks developed during the era of slavery.[24] She highlights an interesting phenomenon that occurred among slave women:

In slavery and in freedom we practiced an alternative style of womanhood. A womanhood that persevered in hardship but reverted overt resistance. A womanhood that celebrated heroism but accepted frailty. A womanhood that could answer a confident and assertive "yes" to the persistent question: "Ar'n't I a woman?"[25]

Gray White found that interdependence among adult female slaves was prevalent; because they performed similar duties on the plantation, they often spent large amounts of time together. They often prepared and ate meals together, cared for the children, cleaned houses, and worked together in the fields. Therefore, slave women frequently developed bonds that resulted in the development of their own female culture.

Patricia Hill Collins's work maintains that black women's social networks remain a vital part of their existence.[26] Collins claims that black women's networks give rise to the creation of "safe spaces"—"social spaces where Black women speak freely."[27] She argues that those spaces are created and maintained in black women's lives through their informal relationships, their cultural traditions, and the voices of black female authors. Collins argues that this type of support provides a realm in which black women are safe and empowered through processes of self-defining, consequently aiding them in resisting dominant negative ideologies. If claims of disappearing social ties were accurate, surely black women would be affected by the disappearance.

However, the literature reveals that even with the multiple forms of oppression that black women experience in this country, social networks continue to be one of their most utilized resources. Be they familial ties or fictive kin, social networks appear to be just as valuable as they were during the era of slavery.[28] The accounts that follow substantiate the importance of black women's networks, particularly how these networks operate in relation to the suicide paradox.

## Our Unyielding Commitment to Others

As previously noted, social integration appears to reduce the probability of suicidal behavior, particularly in the case of black women.[29] So how does a black woman's involvement in close-knit relationships counteract notions of suicide? Black women's testaments of their unyielding commitment to others within their networks were common in my study. The women generally understood that they needed to play a unique role within their associations.

Black women's long-standing experiences with gender and racial oppression have resulted in an internalized set of cultural norms and beliefs that reinforce their commitment to other members of their network. Consequently, black women understand how vital they are to the survival of the black family. Research highlights racial differences among blacks and whites in the frequency of contact and the size of social networks. Blacks report having a smaller number of network members, more frequent contact with those in their networks, and more blood family members in their networks compared to their white counterparts.[30] As a result, black women's networks provide network members with a sense of support, and reinforce racialized and gendered messages that strongly discourage suicidal behaviors among black women.

### *They're Counting on Me*

Several of the women in the study expressed concerns that taking their own life would ultimately mean leaving behind their families and friends. They indicated that no longer being present meant that they would be unable to follow through on the commitments that they had made, and that the thought of disappointing friends and family was often too much for them to bear. Along these lines, Nina conveyed her belief of why it is uncommon for a black woman to take her own life:

> Black women just feel like they have to keep on going, like not being present is just not an option; whether it's for children or for the sake of other people, we have to be present. I have support structures in place, and so even if I thought about suicide, I just feel like if I was really feeling low, I have people who love me, whether it's my friends or family, that I could turn to.

Some years prior to this interview, Nina experienced the suicide of a close friend. She disclosed that learning of his suicide sent an unbelievable shock through her—so much so that the mere thought of causing that kind of pain to her friends or family members was unfathomable.

Kyla revealed that in her family, unlike the boys and young men, she was taught at a very young age that she would need to acquire the necessary skills to contribute something to the family's pool of resources. Failure was not an option for the young women in Kyla's family; achieving the

American Dream was necessary so that these women could assist and invest back in the family. Kyla reported,

> I look at how the men in my family are with stressful situations, or with even the slightest bit of a veer from the path that they think they should be on. They instantly give up. Or they can run to a safe zone, which is usually one of my aunts' houses. Whereas the women in the family, we didn't have the luxury of running home to momma. Like, we were always forced, well, we were *expected* to make it. We were expected to get over it. We were expected to succeed regardless.

This sink-or-swim mentality directed toward female family members taught Kyla the importance of being present to assist her family members in need. She also noted that the males in her family were often seen as more unpredictable than the females. Consequently, the female family members were encouraged to situate themselves in a manner where they could offer support for their entire family if need be. Kyla credited this frame of thinking for black women's low likelihood to commit suicide. She believed that contemporary black family dynamics have resulted in less reliance on black men. Therefore, in relation to Kyla's perceptions of suicide, she deemed the act of suicide incredibly selfish:

> For me, I would consider it [suicide] selfish, not in terms of other people but for my personal life because I know how much I would be missed. I know how much that would hurt my family. I know that my mom would not be able to rebound from that. I know that she would not be able to handle that. And I could just imagine the strain that it would put on my immediate family—my mom, my brother, my dad—and I wouldn't want to do that to them in any way.

Kyla's family viewed her decisions as affecting the entire family, so the thought of taking her own life was highly undesirable. Living up to her family's expectations was very important to Kyla, and she took great pride in her strong sense of interdependence.

Participants' narratives revealed another interesting dynamic: they were too busy caring for others to contemplate suicide, thus, they perceived the act as inconceivably selfish. For example, Terri attributed the rarity of suicide among black women to their high levels of external responsibilities:

> Black women don't kill themselves because they have too many responsibilities, having to hold up family and, you know, all these other things that are on the shoulders of a black woman. Who's going to take care of these things if we are gone?

When I probed Terri to further explain what she meant by "too many responsibilities," she asserted that black women's responsibilities are endless. She then asked me for a brief moment to deliberate on a way to verbalize the breadth of black women's responsibilities to others. She ultimately concluded that the word *everything* worked best to describe what black women are responsible for in their day-to-day lives.

Along these same lines, Ava revealed that her commitment to her circle of networks had directly affected her perceptions of suicide:

> I think traditionally, in the past, African American women have been the foundation of most families, and I think there's that commitment, that "I have to be or I have to follow through with things" . . . and I think that's not the case for white males or for men in general. I think that men do what needs to be done and women do what needs to and should be done, and so our plate is always full. Because we just don't do—we go beyond. . . .
>
> I feel like I always am involved in something. I'm always responsible for something or someone. I'm always doing something and yeah, I'm very committed to the things that I say I'm going to do . . . and so to take [my] life would mean that I would not be following through on a commitment that I made to someone else or a project or something like that. I've always been engaged in something and yeah, I knew I would follow through, I always have a plan for the future.

Ava's devotion to those around her was key in shaping her perceptions of suicide. In direct response to the question "Have you ever considered suicide?" Ava plainly stated, "No . . . I'm too busy." Both Terri's and Ava's accounts revealed the multifaceted ways in which black women's high degree of interdependence operates. Here we not only see high levels of commitment to their social networks, but also that black women's "busyness" creates a sense of tunnel vision. As a result, there is little time to give thought to anything outside of daily responsibilities.

Alisha's response to this topic was a powerful one, revolving around single motherhood. After leaving an abusive spouse, Alisha took on the role of primary caregiver for her children. She said,

> If you are a single mother . . . my children were my life, you see what I'm saying? My children were my life, so I had to be the mother, the father, and all those things to my children. So in order for my children to survive, I had to survive. Those babies depended on me, break me down, beat me up, black my eye, bloody my nose, it don't make no difference, I have to be here.

Black women are more likely to be single mothers than any other racial group,[31] and research suggests single motherhood serves as a protective factor against suicide for black women.[32] Though the research offers little insight on how motherhood operates as a protective factor among black women, Collins's work offers us preliminary insight. Historically the notion of black motherhood in mainstream society has been subjected to close scrutiny. Black mothers are often viewed through the stereotypical lens of whites, resulting in negatively fabricated images. Images such as the "welfare queen," a woman who practices promiscuity, an overweight matriarch, or even a mammy or a mule invade Americans' minds, and the authenticity of these images is rarely questioned.[33]

Consequently, black mothers have come to reconstruct the meaning of black motherhood through various forms of safe spaces (friend and family interactions, formal organizations, etc.). Within the black community it is believed that the child serves as a catalyst for self-definition, self-valuation, and individual empowerment. Thus, motherhood among black women has become a symbol of power and a particularly empowering experience. Alisha's perspectives on suicide are uncompromising. She revealed that there was no scenario she could fathom that would trigger her to have suicidal thoughts. Overall, she perceived suicide to be the "coward's way out."

Alisha also told a story that illustrated how a close friend provided her with psychological motivation, even when dealing with a terminal illness:

> Some situations that happen in our life are not for you. They're for those around you. And what do I mean by that? I had a girlfriend that had breast cancer. She went through it; I mean, she was my Sunday school teacher, she never missed a Sunday at Sunday school. . . . Going through her breast cancer, she had had a breast removed. She never missed a Sunday school day, not a Sunday teaching her class. So I tell her all the time, her going through [that] was not for her. She was just the instrument that God used in order to give me the strength.

Alisha added that her friend's battle with breast cancer helped her to manage stressful situations, and she looked forward to returning the favor someday. She ended by saying, "How can you leave behind someone [speaking of the friend] like that, especially by killing yourself?" Alisha believed suicide to be an extremely selfish act. She attributed black women's overall selfless way of life as fundamental in explaining their infrequent suicidal behavior.

These narratives illustrate that women's devotion to those around them creates a sense of accountability and responsibility. These findings suggest that black women deem their networks critical to their day-to-day survival, and their selfless devotion to others contributes to their low rate of suicide.

## They Got My Back

Despite the fact that black women are often portrayed negatively at a societal level, their positions within their social networks are highly regarded, and black women's position within the black community serves as a medium for positive reinforcement, which thereby counters suicidal tendencies. Terri illustrated this point with the following:

> I think there is a general appreciation for black women within our community, but in society we are not necessarily held up as the highest of all races. However, I think within the black community, black women are very appreciated. Like, you know, their body image is a great thing. More women are getting advanced degrees, so we have this, you know, feeling about ourselves; we are more confident. And I'm sure black women still see all these negative images of themselves or whatever, but it's also being offset by, you know, the likes from black men and other black women.

I think even more recently, women have become more comfortable with telling another woman that, you know, she's great, she looks good and things like that. So, I think black women are held up high within the community and even woman to woman. I think that's important in explaining our suicide rate.

Though many black women see themselves as essential to their communities, my study suggests that they perceive commitments and responsibilities to their networks as a two-way street. Many of the study participants understood the importance of giving, but they regarded receiving as equally important. For example, when asked, "What protects black women from suicide?" Nina answered,

> It sounds corny to say, but the first thing that came to mind was the word *sisterhood*. . . . I feel like in the end, when it really is like a crucial time and you're really down and out, I think that most black women always still have that girlfriend in their corner or they have a go-to person. Someone that will say, "let me hold you down for a couple of days. I got you." You know, I just feel like everybody still has that one person that can support them if the chips are really, really, really down. So I think that that really matters a lot when it comes to dealing with challenges.

Ava shared similar experiences with black women:

> I think for African American women, you know, it's just having a girlfriend and [people] that you loosely define as, you know, friends, professional mentors, and relatives that you know . . . they're your group, you call them. You bounce things off the wall, you vent, you relax; I think it's that outlet, that network that helps us.

It is important to note that Terri's, Nina's, and Ava's accounts of what protects black women from suicide make no mention of utilizing mental-health treatment. Research has long shown that people of color are less likely than whites to seek professional counseling, and more likely to seek "therapy" from informal networks. In a national study, researchers found that black women were more comfortable speaking with a friend or family member, followed by a spiritual leader, followed by another member of their community; doctors and social workers ranked relatively low on the list. These results were relatively consistent among both abused and non-abused African American women.[34]

The black women's discussions of their protective factors mirrored the wider body of research that suggests blacks in general are less likely than whites to seek mental-health treatment.[35] My study affirms black women's views on the importance of their social networks to maintaining their sense of well-being. For example, Donna admitted that she was not very likely to seek professional help to cope with life stressors. Instead, she reported that she would seek emotional support from her "sister friends." She provided the following insight into how a good friend helped her get through difficult times:

> A lot of African American women are not willing to openly go to a psychiatrist if they are having any problems. We pretty much have the, I guess, you could say the girlfriend connection, or as me and my sister say, our gloating box [chuckles], which is where if I'm having problems or I have had a bad day or I have something on my mind, I call my sister and I gloat like, look, this is what went wrong today and you know, da da da da, and my husband didn't take out the trash and our children aren't doing what they're supposed to do, and then she does the same for me, and once we get off the phone, it's like it's gone, we've moved on.... So you're not ... you're not taking baggage with you day to day. You're pretty much finding that one person you can talk to that's just going to listen to you and say, "You know, I understand." And then she says, "Well, let me tell you about my day," and then pretty much after about an hour of conversation, we've forgotten about all the bad that happened that day and we kind of move on.

Similar to Donna, Katherine pointed out that relationships with friends and family are fundamental to avoiding life's pitfalls. She stated, "We have close-knit families and we can go to them for help before it gets to the point where we start thinking about taking our own life."

Ceva also credited the support of her friends and family as a key factor in helping her keep things in perspective during stressful times:

> It's just a support system, somebody that can make you laugh about the situation, somebody that might've gone through the situation themselves

and they just say, "Hey, I made it through. I've been on the other side." So it's that support, the fact that you're not alone.

These narratives show that social networks play a significant role in helping black women cope with life challenges. The vast majority of the women affirmed that their networks serve multiple purposes. Nearly all participants perceive black women's networks as a vital buffer against suicide. Black women's responsibilities within their networks are at times unrelenting; yet, during troubling times, the women have various measures in place to mitigate their stressors. This finding then leads to the following question: *If strong social networks serve as a buffer against suicide for black women, does a lack of such networks create a risk factor?* This question is explored in the next section.

## Lack of Adequate Social-Network Support as a Risk Factor

Because incidents of suicide among African American women are so infrequent, research examining risk factors for this group is very limited. However, just as strong social networks are believed to provide a buffer against suicide, many scholars have discovered that inadequate social support systems seem to increase the risk of suicidal behavior among African American women.[36]

Participants in this study clearly showed that black women rely heavily on the support of their networks, and the accumulation of stressors that black women face causes them to seek levels of support that are often unmatched elsewhere. Their high levels of interconnectedness seem to lessen the likelihood of suicidal behavior. However, participants revealed that without adequate support, feelings of isolation and hopelessness can quickly surface.

Despite black women's low suicide-completion rate, I asked participants to speak to what they believed increases black women's risks. More specifically, I asked each woman to discuss under what circumstances she thought that she or another black woman would turn to suicide as a solution to her problems. The commonality among the responses was that they would have to be in a place where they felt an overwhelming sense of hopelessness.

Often the sense of hopelessness that they spoke of coincided with little contact with friends and family.

For example, Hilldreth recalled the suicide attempt of a black woman from her community who had fallen on hard times and lacked family and community support:

> Well, I just remember her having a sense of hopelessness. She had just lost her job. She had family issues. Her and her boyfriend had broken up and it felt like everything was kind of going down the drain all at the same time. Instead of coping with the reality of what was put forth in front of her, she felt like she would be doing her family a favor by eliminating herself from the picture. So, she took a bottle of pills, but her mom showed up to the house not long afterwards, so she was able to get her to the hospital in time.

Hilldreth believed that the lack of social support in the woman's life was central to her suicide attempt. She claimed that the woman was sending out a cry for help, and once she got the attention of her friends and family, she was able to begin down the path of recovery.

Ceva also referred to a sense of hopelessness as being the reason black women may contemplate suicide:

> Just feeling like they are at the bottom of the barrel and they have nowhere else to go. They might have given up on God, their friends and family are either deceased or nonexistent. They might have some kind of illness or . . . I don't know, they just feel like there's not any hope or any reason for them to be alive.

Ceva then pondered what would likely need to occur in her own life before she could think of attempting suicide:

> I don't really think I would get to that point. I would have to be homeless, nobody around, and really sick with a terminal disease. All of those things will have to occur at the same time for me to even consider it.

Delilah echoed the notion that a sense of hopelessness would perhaps drive a black woman to contemplate suicide:

> I would think having come to a point where you think you can't make it happen, or you lose your job, and you can't seem to get another. You don't know where to go. You're homeless. You know, you've depleted all of your funds, and you don't know what to do; and not to mention you have no family, children, or what have you. I believe it's that . . . feeling of hopelessness and helplessness. I think that would probably be something that would drive a black woman . . . to think of suicide.

Another factor that emerged in the narratives revolved around how historical and contemporary bouts of discrimination experienced by the black family have resulted in the need for a strong sense of social connectedness, and while this connectedness among black women and their families accounts for low the suicide rate, lack of connectedness likely accounts for increased risk. For example, Donna stated the following:

> Black women have grown up from a background that we've come from little or nothing, so we had to have strong family support. So a lot of black women wouldn't consider suicide unless they were off from their family and they couldn't get back to their family. But most of us, you know, once you have a family and you have people that support you and people that lean on you, you're not going to do anything to just leave them alone.

Robin concurred that this connectedness was critical. She told the story of a friend who was dealing with some very challenging times and expressed concern that the woman seemed to have suicidal tendencies, particularly because she lacked family connections:

> Family is very important to African American women. . . . Well, you know, I worry about . . . I have a friend who has really been faced with some challenges since the economy tanked. She has lost her job after more than twelve years in a position. She was a director of a major program, and she has not just been able to find a job and it's been over six months. And I hear it in her voice and it worries me because she doesn't have strong family connections.
>
> So I keep in contact with her and it worries me how she's handling that stress in her life. She teases me all the time when I can't get in touch with her and she says, "It's because my feet are hanging over the bridge." I mean, it's a joke that we've been saying to each other for years when we

can't get in touch with each other. She said, "I'm hanging, my feet are hanging over the bridge. Where are you?" Lately, I have started to take her more seriously, so I do my best to make sure that she has the support from me that she needs.

Participants repeatedly brought up the notion of lack of support as a risk factor for suicide. Kyla provided the following insight regarding what factors might put women at risk:

> I think for women that don't have a very strong relationship with a mentor or someone that guides them, be it family or outside of family. I think that the feeling of "it takes a whole community to raise a child" is still very prevalent in the black community. So I think women that don't have that rock, that one person that they can always talk to or a very, very good friend, especially sisters, like we call our girls when something goes down [laughing] . . . if we don't have that then that definitely leaves us extremely vulnerable to anything that comes our way. If we already have this weak foundation in terms of how society sees us and we don't have that extra pillar to help support us then as problems start to mount, it will definitely push you down.

Similar to Kyla, Terri stated that a black woman who has been ousted from her friends, family, and community would most definitely be at risk for suicidal behavior, herself included:

> I'd probably say black women not having a strong support system, because I think that's what really helps me the most, because I mentioned that me being . . . like the black sheep or being, you know, discommunicated from my family, would make me want to commit suicide potentially. And I think if I didn't have the support system that I do have, it might have been something I considered. Especially like when I became Buddhist and my mom cut me off, I think it would have been very hard for me. So I think that it helps out to have somebody to reassure you that you are great or you should not feel alone, just to have somebody that says, "I love you and I care about you."

Clara provided a unique perspective as she talked about how she had attempted to end her life when she was in her twenties. Her marriage was coming to an end and she found herself depressed. Clara admits to consuming a large amount of alcohol and then taking "a bunch of pills." She then proceeded to take a hot bath, where her husband at the time later found her unresponsive. She was rushed to the hospital, where they were able to pump her stomach and stabilize her. According to Clara, she really did not want to die; she simply wanted to end the stress and the pain. She is now in a place where she is confident that she would never attempt suicide again, and she credited her recovery to group-therapy sessions that she attended, along with the help of a close friend with whom she reconnected during group therapy. Clara had learned firsthand how critical social networks are to black women's survival:

> I find this with most African American women, that they have these very extensive networks of friends who are there to provide a context when you talk about stress. To basically relieve this stress through talking with others. . . . For an African American woman to indeed commit suicide would mean that that whole support network just simply disappears for whatever reason. I think since it is so important to African American women who had to struggle so much . . . they find themselves in a situation for whatever reason, psychological, sociological, in which they are unable to quickly reestablish. I mean, it's like sort of being in limbo. And I can think about my youngest sister; I have no idea how she could survive without that network of friends—that . . . that absolute necessary daily connection, almost hourly connection [laughs].

These narratives confirm participants' strong conviction that a lack of adequate social networks puts black women at risk for suicide. These women's beliefs are based on personal observations and experiences and, as such, contribute greatly to the literature on black women's risk factors for suicide. Based on these findings, healthcare professionals must consider the unique role of black women's networks in their lives when instituting treatment and suicide-prevention programs in the black community.[37]

## Summary

Despite prominent race theorists' arguing that many of the black family's social ties and networks are weakening or disappearing,[38] contemporary literature on black women tells a different story. It appears that social networks continue to be a primary source of strength for black women. Black women's networks remain essential to their physical and psychological well-being. Much research shows that black women rely heavily on their networks to redefine and reinforce positive images of themselves. Black women's commitment to their social networks plays a significant role in their perceptions of suicide. In fact, my findings suggest that it is these close interactions that create and reinforce well-defined beliefs about the notion of suicide.

Among my respondents, high levels of interdependence are associated with low levels of suicide acceptability. Respondents frequently stated that because of their commitment to friends and family members, leaving those people behind was simply not an option. Significantly, all of my respondents noted that the support of friends and family members was a critical source of their resilience, and they overwhelmingly indicated that a lack of such support could increase their risk for suicidal tendencies. Simply put, multifaceted layers of emotional, physical, and social support materialize into black women's infrequent use of suicide as a solution to their problems. Black women recognize that lack of support places them at increased risk for suicidal behavior—so much so that they actively seek out support networks to avoid such behavior.

## Chapter 5
## Only the Strong Survive
### Notions of Strength, Resiliency, and Suicide

*Because that's where my strength comes from. My strength comes from my trials that are behind me; that gives me strength to face those that are before me. So life teaches you those things. If you don't buckle under. . . . Because we as black women know that only the strong survive.*
—Alisha[1]

Understanding black women's perceptions regarding why their suicide rate has remained consistently low is critical to understanding how black women fare in a world where they would seem to be just as suicide prone as white males. This chapter reveals that black women have constructed a fairly clear image of themselves, an image of resiliency. We see in Alisha's opening quote that she has survived many of the challenges life has brought her way. She credits her current and past struggles as a black woman as her primary means of building strength. Alisha expressed to me that the "trials" she spoke of not only increase her capacity to survive challenging times, but also strengthen many other black women as well.

Alisha's comments were mirrored several times throughout my study. In fact, just under half of the women cited their ability to survive even the most grueling circumstances as a major factor in black women's low suicide rate. Regardless of the origin of their stress, black women filtered their experiences through their perceptions of themselves as resilient. This chapter provides insight into how such thought processes often materialize, thereby affecting the act or, in this case, the resolve to not act. To further explain black women's perceptions on the matter, participants were asked to discuss what they believed contributes to black women's low suicide rate. The following narratives reveal the ways in which black women frame notions of strength and weakness, one's social position on the racial and gender hierarchy, and the experiences of their forefathers in this country as explanations for the black-white suicide paradox.

### How We Acquired Our "Strength"

> *Maybe, well . . . I've been through a lot, so if I was going to commit suicide, I would have been dead a long time ago. So I guess things like not having a job or the kids just stressing me out don't make me want to give up. It's just what life takes us through and we [black women] know that we have to be stronger.*
>
> —Justine[2]

So, how do black women's perceptions of strength relate to low suicide completion and attempt rates? According to my participants, one explanation stems from black women's sense that they, and the American blacks that came before them, were born into a struggle. African Americans in this country have historically endured extreme emotional, social, physical, and psychological hardships. The literature thus far has established that black women disproportionately continue to face dilemmas in virtually every arena of their lives.[3] Though these encounters have certainly had an effect on the physical and psychological health of these women,[4] it appears that their experiences, gained from both historical and present-day oppression, have taken on the role of a safeguard against the occurrence of suicide ideation. Thus, in response to discussions of why black women's suicide rates are low, the narratives from this study demonstrate that black women depend on multiple resources to endure the challenges they face. In this chapter I discuss black women's continued acknowledgement of the vital role that history has played in shaping present-day African American self-identities and perceptions of suicide.

## We Stand on the Shoulders of Those Who Came Before Us

A significant finding of this study was that every single participant measured the magnitude of her present-day struggles within a historical context, thereby lessening the psychological impact of the crisis at hand. Each account presented exemplifies how the participants' individual identities are influenced by collective memory. Nora, for instance, argues that objects such as pictures, stories, and living and deceased relatives serve as a channel to chronicle past experiences to those of the present.[5]

Black women's perception that they come from a struggle played an essential role in the way the participants perceived the notion of suicide. These powerful narratives were in direct response to the question "Why are black women's suicide rates significantly lower than the rest?" For example, Cheryl drew on an example from more than three centuries ago. Her account of the Middle Passage and slavery was presented within a framework indicating that if black women could survive these grueling circumstances, then she could classify them as "survivors":

> I think the reason why, it's because black women, in my opinion, are survivors. We have survived the Middle Passage. We have survived slavery. We have survived—what's the word with that? When I say slavery, the last 300 years . . . the master can come in and rape us and impregnate us and we've had to suck it up and I go back to that word and that just means you have to just tough it out and you have to . . . it's called tough luck. You just have to survive it, so even if you have to endure daily rapes and you have to endure your children being taken from you and being sold to another plantation . . . our ancestors had to live for the children they did have, so I think . . . I'm getting spiritual and then maybe this is crazy, but I think that spirit lives on in us. I really think that essence lives within us and that is why we'll continue to endure—because of our background and because of what we've gone through, coming from the mother country, coming from the Ivory Coast or West Africa or wherever we have, wherever we happen to come from.

Cheryl shared experiences of how racial and gendered oppression have contributed to the sense of strength that black women embody. They consider themselves to be survivors rather than incompetent as suggested by deceiving media images.[6] Cheryl provided insight into how black women perceive these hardships. There appears to be a segment of black women's lives that external circumstances cannot alter. Therefore, whether it is rape, the loss of a family member, or whatever it may be, their sense of collective memory and endurance has shaped their perceptions of themselves and what they can cope with.

Ava, a black woman in her mid-thirties, admits that she continues to draw on the strength gained by blacks during the civil-rights movement:

> The civil-rights movement has meant a lot to me. To see black people's ability to basically go through the tortures, the beatings, the abductions, the assaults by police; we watch videos, we've seen the stories and blacks, especially black women, say, "Well, if they can do that, then surely I can just tolerate this." And I think we have become desensitized to trauma, to unfairness, and we feel through it all that we are just expected to tolerate it.

Although Ava referenced a more recent event, she too used the historical oppression of African Americans as a gauge of her capability to handle modern-day adversities. Similarly, Hilldreth (the youngest of the four women discussed in this section) and Delilah both referenced historical events as a source of black women's long-standing resiliency. Neither referenced a particular event, but instead the women were aware of the history of oppression that black women have faced. Hilldreth and Delilah both made use of similar terminology to express their views on black women's responses to long-term oppression. Hilldreth labeled this response "accustomed to getting the short end of the stick," and Delilah remarked that black women get to "a place where it [long-term exposure to adversity] hardens us." Both illustrate black women's perspectives on coping with life's difficulties. Hilldreth said,

> Black women's suicide rates are low because as black women, we have become accustomed to being oppressed; it dates back to slavery. We were oppressed for a very, very long time, so we know how to handle stress. We know how to handle things that come our way. . . . If we lose our

jobs or if someone hurts us in any way, we know how to handle that because we have been accustomed to getting the short end of the stick for so many years. So when you are used to living that kind of life, what could make us kill ourselves?

And Delilah expressed,

> I think it is because we as black women face controversies early in our lives and probably throughout our lives. And sometimes when something happened to another race, it is probably more devastating, I think, for them than it would be for us because we are used to facing controversies. We face a lot of things and so we're able to cope with things that perhaps bring us displeasure, you know, at an early age. So I think that we are more able to handle disappointment because we're accustomed to it. I guess you might say we get to a place that this hardens us and we get used to it. Living this kind of life minimizes the chances that we [black women] would turn to suicide.

These women recognized that historical and modern-day oppressive conditions have helped them to develop philosophies that guide the strategies black women use to navigate through difficult situations.[7] The experiences from which they drew seemed to be ingrained in their consciousness, which plays a significant role in shaping their perceptions about survival and ultimately suicide. The amount of time that has passed since the events referenced (slavery, the civil-rights movement, etc.) appears irrelevant. More importantly, the respondents, regardless of their ages, use these historical occurrences as a constant reminder of the resiliency that has traveled through their bloodlines and will continue to do so for generations to come.

### *We Remain at the Bottom of the Barrel: Black Women's Take on Their Current Social Position*

In "The Psychology of Black Women: Studying Women's Lives in Context," author Veronica Thomas states, "No other group has been victimized by hegemonic domination and located within the hierarchical power structure as black women have in American society."[8] Because of the severity of their oppression, black women offer a one-of-a-kind perspective unfamiliar to any other group, including black men, white women, and all other nonblack women.[9] The complex lives of black women become even more apparent when defining themselves and the black race as long-suffering. Participants' narratives revealed that black women are very much aware of their racialized, gendered status in US society.[10] Not only are they aware of their lower social position, but they consider themselves to be at the bottom of the social hierarchy.[11] In regard to the low suicide rate among black women, Katherine bluntly declared that black women's social position in the hierarchy ultimately prepares them for whatever challenges life might bring:

> The black women that I know are brought up [believing] that suicide is definitely not an option. We came from poverty and stuff like that anyway, so we came from the lowest; you can't go too much lower when you come from that. You know what I'm saying? I think that has a lot to do with it.

Tasha, too, acknowledged that there appears to be a hierarchical arrangement of racial groups and genders in US society. Similar to Katherine, rather than being discouraged about her stance, Tasha believes that these experiences have made her stronger:

> I see kind of a social and financial scale, but I think black women have a lot of issues that we have to face, one, by being women and then by being black. We have a lot of things we have to struggle against. But I think the experience I have had strengthened me. You start out fighting in a sense, not necessarily physically fighting, but you have to struggle just to survive.

Cheryl's discussion of suicide and the social position of black women brought forth an interesting notion. Cheryl claims that just as black women have remained at the bottom of the racial-gender hierarchy, white men and to some extent white women have a stake at the top:

> I think there's a greater pressure on white people, both white men and white women. There are lower expectations for black people, especially black women, and I think that in a way, it's harmful because when people expect less of us, it affects how we perform, but by the same token, when you have lesser expectations, you have more breathing room. I think that

leaves room for whites to consider suicide more so than black women and African Americans in general.

She maintained that lower societal expectations for blacks to succeed likely result in less pressure. Whites are considered to be the yardstick in Cheryl's example, which fits directly into notions of the black/white paradigm. Sociologist Joe Feagin asserts that the exploitation of blacks was institutionalized and lasted for at least four centuries. Whites have dominated nonwhites from a previously established and highly embedded system of antiblack racism. The hierarchy consisted of whites on top and blacks on bottom, and that was the measuring stick.[12]

Katherine, Tasha, and Cheryl each recognize the unique social standing of black women in the United States. They accept the fact that they have inherited a level of disadvantage that is virtually impossible to overcome. Nevertheless, the women see this phenomenon as a contributing factor to black women's sense of resiliency.

### We Can't Miss What We Never Had

Women's discussions of their hard pasts and contemporary struggles brought to the surface an additional way in which notions of long-term suffering ward off thoughts of suicidal behavior. The notion that people cannot miss what they've never had was mentioned by multiple women as directly related to black women's low suicide rate. Several women mentioned that the low rate could be related to black women's long-term exposure to material and economic want. The women perceived that sudden loss of prestige, status, wealth, or material possessions can significantly increase a person's risk for suicide, particularly among whites. What was also interesting about this notion was that black women, regardless of their socioeconomic level, deemed this significant. On the topic of lack of money, Karen stated,

> Well, to me black women have always had a level of stress to deal with that would overwhelm most white women, black men, or white men, and I think because of all the pressures and stuff that has been put on them [black women] to, like a lot of them, be single parents or to be head of household. A lot of them saw no option of leaving the family. Suicide means that you would leave these people behind. So that's just not an option. We [black women] can deal with what's going on in the world.

> So, with the bailouts and money problems, we're unmoved. Well, if you never had a lot of money, those problems really don't affect you as much, because you're not really going to lose anything because you never had it. What you don't have, you can't lose.

Connections between one's economic standing and suicide rates are not an entirely new phenomenon. Steven Stack conducted a systematic review of suicide-related sociological literature over a fifteen-year period; the trends highlighted an inverse relationship between suicide risk and social class standing.[13] Yet black women's accounts appear to contrast with the literature in this area.

Tina, for example, acknowledges the economic disparities between whites and African Americans, but Tina claims that we must focus on the relative breakdown of losing versus not possessing in the first place:

> I am of black descent, African American descent. We come in with a struggle. We're pretty much born or the majority of us are born into this cycle of struggle. So when we're faced with adversity, I think it has become part of our nature as well as our DNA, to fight back a little longer, a little harder. You can't miss anything you've never had. The majority of us haven't had that kind of life. So when we don't get it, it's not a big deal, but to have had it and lost it, that's a whole different ball game.

Along the same lines, Tasha provided a magnificent example of how viewing life in these terms helps black women avoid suicidal behavior:

> Things have gotten pretty bad in my life in the past. There are many people who have a lot more than I do as far as finances, good [physical] shape. There are people that are better off than I am and there are people that are worse off than I am and just realizing, okay, I may not have a size 9 body, but I do not have a size 22 either. I may not have the best job, but I have a job that allows me to spend time with my family. So just being able to not just look at the negatives in life, but being able to appreciate the blessings.

Tasha uses the experiences of others as a lens for viewing her own circumstances. She shared that she had thoughts of suicide as a teenager, but never acted on them. She had a rough childhood, but she expressed that these challenging times strengthened her. Instead of focusing on the things that she lacks, Tasha now lives by the mantra "this too shall pass." This type of mentality was common among the women in the study. Regardless of how difficult things got for them, there was the common perception that things could be worse. It was their way of drawing attention to the silver lining often overlooked by others. Thus, be it making the best of their social positions, drawing from the strength of their ancestors, or keeping a positive spin on life, black women's narratives expose exactly how varying sources of strength affect their perceptions of the suicide paradox.

## Seeing Ourselves as Resilient and Strong

Pathological portrayals of black women in the literature pay particular attention to the negative mental-health effects caused by issues such as substance abuse, dysfunctional family circumstances, and single-parenthood issues.[14] Contemporary misrepresentations of black women in the media are overwhelming. In fact, 97 percent of the black women in the Charissse Jones and Kumea Shorter-Gooden study say that they acknowledge negative stereotypes in the media, and 80 percent claim that they have personally been affected by these racist and sexist assumptions.[15] Patricia Hill Collins asserts that ever-evolving controlling images of black women pervade the media, but despite the fact that there has been a surge in black professional women, contemporary images fail to reveal this change. Collins goes on to say that modern-day mammies have become "black bitches" (angry, loud, and aggressive) contrasted on the other end of the racial spectrum with images of bad mothers.[16]

Alice Deck demonstrates how food and ethnicity have been used as an apparatus of discrimination toward people of color. She illustrates this point by exposing prominent images of black women in American culture, such as in novels, films, ads, and TV shows, dating back 100 years. Many of the images in the advertisements are said to portray black women in a masculine way. The rationale behind these acts was to make the white homemaker feel safe while her husband was away. In other words, as long as mammy was around, she could act as the man of the house, thereby protecting the white woman.[17]

The notion of the jezebel was also a negative image of black women heavily circulated in the media. The jezebel was framed as a sex-crazed black woman. Deborah Gray White argues that the image of the jezebel maintained among white men resulted in centuries of sexual abuse and rape. Thus, it was not uncommon for black women at times to have to deal with abuse from both the white master and his wife. Images of the sapphire emerged after slavery ended. The sapphire was framed as a domineering female who consumes men while taking control of them. That stereotype was fairly closely aligned with conceptions of the matriarch of the black family.[18]

However, the accounts of my study's participants illuminated an entirely different perspective on stereotypical notions of the black woman as "strong." In response to the question of why black women's suicide rate is consistently low, several attributed this phenomenon to black women's "declaration of strength" promoting notions of resiliency and the ability to survive some of life's most challenging circumstances. The accounts provided in this study reveal not only black women's resiliency, but also their vulnerability. Their narratives are far from complacent. Instead, they demonstrate a sense of cultural pride in the fact that black women have been able to thrive under the bleakest of circumstances.

## We've Learned to Adapt

In short, almost half of the women credited the unique ability to make a way out of no way as a cause for the low suicide rate. This was an entirely unique finding. The majority of my participants admitted that regardless of what they are facing, they almost never lose hope that they will ultimately overcome the challenge. These discussions brought out a variety of paralinguistic cues that the women themselves explained as excitement and gratitude.

One of the advantages to conducting face-to-face interviews is that body language and other paralinguistic cues can aid in interpreting data.[19] According to Kikuo Maekawa, one's mental attitude or intention is often conveyed during speech. This was very much the case when discussions of black women and strength emerged in the interviews. This topic evoked amplified voices, with the women at times standing up, and even intense statements, almost to the point of tears. These were by no means negative emotions, but instead were prideful and affirmative. It also became apparent that black women hold other black women to the same standards they hold themselves. For instance, Tina proclaimed,

> We're just not single parents . . . we go in thinking, "He [the man] might not be here forever, so I got to do this." I've heard in several movies, "black women don't do what they *want* to do, they do what they *need* to do." So, I think we've been raised with that type of mentality. So, whether it comes from family, friends, life experience, or whatever, we're just able to bounce back. I mean, African American women carry the burden compared to men. In our community, if we don't have a screwdriver, we grab a butter knife; we improvise. So, we look at other avenues to handle things, to take care of things, to get the job done.

After making those comments, Tina paused for a moment to process what she'd just said. I could see that she was in deep thought. I asked her, "What came up for you in that moment?" She informed me that despite the challenges black women have to overcome, she's proud to be part of a culture that "knows how to make a way out of no way." Tina was delighted at black women's ability to bounce back. She associated black women's low incidence of suicide with their strength and their capacity to get creative in the effort to simplify things. Although Tina did contemplate suicide during a difficult time of her life, she expressed that absolutely nothing could cause her to consider it now.

Justine also spoke confidently about black women's ability to persevere through difficult times:

> Even though our life gets tough, we're not going to take our life. We'd take somebody else's life, but not our own. It just comes back to us having that strong sense of perseverance. Just what we already know, what we already been through, as a black woman—we just know how to survive. We know how to make bread and butter at the same time, we know how to run a household and deal with every other situation that's coming into play. I . . . lost everything in Hurricane Katrina: my house, my clothes, and my car. And not once have I considered suicide. We've been through too much as a people for me to go out like that.

Like Tina, Justine illustrated that the coping strategies black women have been forced to develop have fostered an increased ability to be innovative with the resources they have access to. In the same way, Alisha confidently boasted that black women are the stronger ones:

> Number one [chuckles], we have been . . . let me see, what do I want to call that? It is a subject or a topic or a course, let's say a course—it is a course that black females are taught early in life, that regardless of the man you may marry you are always the stronger one. Black women are always the stronger ones.

This is a particularly remarkable statement considering the fact that Alisha survived an abusive spousal relationship, has had to cope with her son being sent to prison, and now has full custody over her grandson. She went on to discuss her beliefs on suicide:

> Suicide is the coward's way out. It's the coward's way out. When black women ask God for more strength, when I ask even in my prayers, when I pray and ask for more strength, I'm asking for more trials, I'm asking for more tribulations. So I know still through it all, I'm still going to stand.

Alisha's notion of suicide as a cowardly act affirms other study participants' beliefs regarding an opposition of the strong versus the weak. Despite black women exhibiting the typical associations between oppressive conditions and mental health,[20] suicide appears to be the exception.

Myths of the black "superwoman" are apparent throughout social-science literature. Portrayals of black women as unshakable, overbearing, and masculine can have misleading effects on the way black women perceive themselves. Jones and Shorter-Gooden argue that black women are oftentimes flattered by their reputations of strength and offended at thoughts of being considered overbearing and masculine. Similarly, the narratives of my study reveal not so much that black women brag about their strength, but instead that they acknowledge their increased capacity to survive troubling times because of the racist and sexist society they inherited. Thus, black women's notions of strength are less about blackness being synonymous with strength than about the social environment that required black women to acquire these skills in the first place. Thus, black women learned about the importance of strength from other blacks, but they also learned it from whites. Historically, whites placed blacks into life-threatening social environments in which they were given two options: survive or die. So, how do these notions relate to the black women's perceptions of the suicide paradox? Figure 5.1 illustrates how black women see the role strength has played in their occurrences of suicide.

I propose that black women's perceptions of strength stem from their ancestors' ability to overcome long-term bouts of suffering, coupled with the resiliency that gives them the ability to endure. This results in black women identifying suicide as an unacceptable option. Thus, the unique experiences of black women seem to impact the way they see themselves in relation to suicide. They have come to define themselves as resilient survivors with a sense of purpose, an identity that defies suicide. Throwing in the towel is not an option because, as Alisha stated, "only the strong survive."

## Privileged Social Position + Inability to Cope = Higher Probability of Suicide

One winter afternoon I sat down to have a conversation with a black male family member. We discussed life, politics, and work. During our

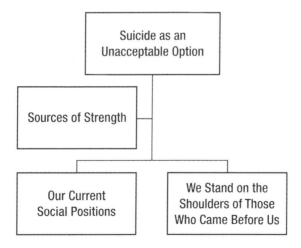

**Figure 5.1 Visual illustration of themes associated with black women's low suicide rates.**

discussions of work, he told me a story about a young coworker about whom he was concerned. A white male confided that he had been having suicidal thoughts. My family member probed the young man for information: "Hey, man, what's got you down?" My family member then told me that the man revealed he had been having a rough weekend.

He was currently living in his parents' basement, and he was annoyed with the fact that his father would not give him any privacy. Whenever he wanted to have friends over, his father would always come down into the basement to monitor their behavior. The young man said, "I just don't know how much more of this I can take. I bet my dad will miss me when I'm gone." Then, he boldly stated, "I should end it all right now!" As anyone would in this type of situation, my family member tried to offer words of wisdom and encouragement. Although they were only new acquaintances, he didn't want this individual to harm himself. My family member went back to work the next day, but this young man was no longer on his shift. To this day he is not sure what happened to him, and he still wonders about him from time to time. My family member thinks the most interesting thing about this situation was that this white male was contemplating suicide over what many would consider an insignificant event. He stated, "White men don't understand what it's like to struggle, especially like blacks do. They're weak."

Black women's narratives revealed similar perceptions. Their stories painted pictures of weak-willed men with very little capacity for struggle. Even more intriguing about this finding was that black women defined themselves and their ability to handle stressful events in complete opposition to white males. Figure 5.2 shows a visual demonstration of black women's perceptions regarding the continuum of strength and weakness in relation to their perceptions of "typical" suicide victims. As the figure shows, perceptions of suicide probability were correlated with this continuum of strength versus weakness. Statistically, black women and white men represent the two extremes when it comes to actual incidents of suicide. More than 90 percent of all suicide deaths occur among white males.[21] Additionally, this can be seen with 2011 age-adjusted rates of 22.6 suicides per 100,000 for white men and 1.8 for black women.[22] The women unmistakably used "strength" in a positive context and "weakness" in a negative one. Their narratives identify social advantages guaranteed to them by virtue of their privileged racial and gender status as a primary explanation for white men's higher suicide-completion rates.

**Figure 5.2** Black women's perceptions of suicide probability among white men and black women.

## *Unmerited Advantages*

The respondents' perceptions of weakness emerged during discussions of black-white rate disparities. In response to the question "Why do you perceive white men's rates to be significantly higher than black women's?" Bridgett, a single woman, shared a childhood memory of a white male committing suicide:

> I remember growing up, it was probably my aunt or someone saying it, we were watching some kind of movie and this white guy was standing on a ledge threatening to jump. He was obviously a big-time executive or something of that nature. He was standing outside of his window; the stocks crashed and they show him jumping out. And I remember my aunt saying, "See, that's what white men do." They would commit suicide because they're not used to living a life that is less than what they expected or felt like they should have in their life.

Although Bridgett was only a child at that time, she never forgot that incident.

Narratives of the women showed that they closely attribute white males' historical lack of suffering as a major role in their higher probability of suicide. Along these same lines, we see similarities in both Delilah's and Sandy's points. Delilah articulated this point nicely:

> Whites are accustomed to having their way or getting what they need, providing for their families, and they are looked at as, "I can do anything," because there are more opportunities available to them in most cases. And when they cannot provide, then they feel like failures, and they feel like they can no longer go on. They just can't cope.

Delilah's remark is indicative of notions of white privilege circulated in social-science literature.[23] Peggy McIntosh's work on white privilege highlights "invisible systems of dominance" that give whites, both men and women, unmerited advantages.[24] White privilege materialized during the periods of legal slavery and legal segregation. In the same way, the notions of privilege were embedded into America's most prominent institutions. Feagin argues that this unstable period in our history bred white racist ideologies and attitudes that were created to maintain and rationalize systems of white privilege.[25] Sandy says,

> Well, I think in a lot of those instances, um, a lot of white men, um, just white families in general, they come from pretty wealthy homes, they have pretty wealthy parents and stuff like that. And I think that when they don't, um, basically live life or become as successful as their parents, I think that there's a lot of pressure on them and they tend to, to just kind of give up on life, unfortunately, and you know, drugs, alcohol, things like that, I'm sure play a big part as well.

Sandy's presumption that white men come from affluent backgrounds implies that she believes that white men are socially and economically privileged. She later mentioned that from her perspective, white men are just unable to cope, and suffering gives rise to strength.

### Born with a Silver Spoon in Their Mouths

Race-based discrimination, prejudice, and oppression are supposedly a thing of the past. Everyone has equal opportunity and access to the American Dream. Therefore, despite the brutal history of the United States, we have finally achieved utopia, a "color-blind" society. Then why are notions of a color-blind society a part of everyday discourse? Many scholars claim that race isn't a thing of the past. They claim that the myth of a color-blind society continues to complicate things. The issue of race seems to be as full of hypocrisy as many other elements of US society. We are race-neutral in theory, but racialized in practice.

Before one can be said to have racial characteristics, we must first be able to identify those characteristics—thus, we are "racing." Racing occurs from the top down, and it involves assigning and denying groups racial identity. John Powell claims that the role the government and the white majority have played in creating and maintaining racialized space (crime, welfare dependency, economic deprivation, joblessness, and so on) is used as a tool to preserve white privilege.[26] Whites' attempts to preserve white space often yield unjust advantages. Bridgett imparted a contemporary example of how she perceives the psychological consequences of white privilege playing out in the lives of whites in a tragic situation:

> Even if I think about like, . . . in the movie *Titanic* . . . there were some people that had committed suicide and I remember . . . a couple of family members had kind of talked about . . . that's just because they're used to having in a sense white privilege so when you feel like you've lost that, kind of like they don't know what to do now because they're so used to living life here at this standard, so if something happens to fall down below that standard it's maybe a major shock.

Bridgett argued that the privileged lives of white men do very little to equip them with how to handle failure or want. We see this again in Hilldreth's narrative; she expressed that white men's elevated social status affords them little tolerance for variation in their lives. Hilldreth believes that white men would rather be dead than poor, whereas blacks would rather be poor than dead, an interesting paradigm comparison.

> Because white men are so accustomed to being elevated to the point of being their own god . . . and they're so used to having that, when they don't have, they don't know how to deal with it because they would rather be dead than be poor or they would rather be dead than be embarrassed in front of their peers, but we [black people] . . . just handle it differently.

White privilege can have damaging effects on non–privilege holders. According to Powell's article "Whites Will Be Whites," whites assert their innocence and demonize others by engaging in discourse that deems the "other" to be undeserving.[27] Powell suggests that privilege on a structural level seeks to normalize or maintain the system. Ceva provided a very thorough explanation of her perception on the privileged background of whites:

Blacks are going to struggle; blacks are just used to existing in economic and social statuses that whites have never been in. So, therefore, when things hit whites versus when things hit blacks there's a difference. So when something such as the Great Depression hits or a recession is going on, we don't feel like, "Oh we're going to die" or "Oh, our livelihood has gone away." We just feel that this is another tough time; we'll make it through.

But for the white people, they don't live with that same knowledge or they don't live with that same awareness like we do. So therefore when a recession happens or when a depression happens, their feelings are hurt. They don't think they're going to live the same life that they lived. They spend a lot of their life on credit. So when their credit runs out, so goes their livelihood, so suicide becomes more of an option.

Ceva's discussion again ties back to black women's perception of strength and weakness related to suicide. Ceva revealed that she believes blacks are used to the disappointment that comes along with not achieving what they set out to; however, she argued that whites "spend a lot of their life on credit," so the loss of this credit (which Ceva equates with privilege) threatens their livelihood.

### Can't Take the Heat

*There are a lot of stresses put on white men to be the best at everything. They have to be the best. If they are not the best then there are issues. They can't tolerate even half of the things that black people can. They are not supposed to be less than us. And I don't think they have the tools to survive it.*

—Kyndall[28]

We have established the fact that the black women's narratives assume white men's weaknesses are associated with long-term exposure to unwarranted privilege; however, black women also perceived white men's weaknesses to be associated with the fact that they buckle under pressure. Similarities between the privilege of the silver spoon and the idea that whites "can't take the heat" provide an interesting contrast. When the women spoke of notions of white privilege, they were referring to the historical and modern-day social environment, whereas in their discussions of people not being able to take the heat, they referred to white men's reactions to the conditions. Nonetheless, perceptions of weakness were incorporated in both, with a presumed outcome of suicide as a result.

Justine is no stranger to life's hardships. She revealed that her move to Texas following Hurricane Katrina had been a stress itself. Besides the stress of leaving behind many of her established networks, she found that Texas has too many rules; to say the least, it is a racist environment. She found a job almost immediately upon arrival, but she and her children have struggled with bouts of prejudice and discrimination since the relocation. When asked to describe her position on suicide disparities between white men and black women, she stated,

> White men . . . that's what they do [suicide]. Whites take their life and nothing don't have to be going on; they can have the best of everything and they'd still take their life. Because when you're looking at the news and they're committing suicide, and you're looking at the news and they're telling you, oh, so and so had this and had that, what's going on in his life? Would you like to know what's playing that big part? Why whites are committing suicide? It's because they have the best of both worlds. They get the benefit of the doubt in everything, and some of them even have the money and the education and you [blacks]. But, just looking at them, they're taking pills or they're taking overdoses with needles or they're hanging and shooting themselves.

Justine has come to terms with the fact that her struggles as a black woman have prepared her to survive whatever society throws her way. Justine's perception of white males' inability to survive even the slightest amount of pressure was unfathomable to her. Tina, a single woman who has achieved middle-class status through her hard work and education, also implied that white men's inability to cope is related to their lack of long-standing struggle. Like Justine, Tina discussed notions of white people's inability to manage life's challenges:

> The Caucasian community, their upbringing and their lifestyle is less stressful than those in the African American community. So, when

something hits them that is on the opposite end of the spectrum, they don't know what to do because that's not something that is consistent in their life. They [whites] were taught about the finances and to save and to do these things in their community, as well as other races other than the black community, but it's like when they lose that, it's just over.

Although Tina contemplated suicide at one time in her life, she argued that she would have never followed through on the thoughts. She finds the act itself absurd. Tasha, a married graduate student, also attributed white men's lack of experience with oppression as an underlying cause of their weakness:

> White men have a lot of things that are working for them just by virtue of the fact that they are white and they are males, and so they have more advantages. I hate to generalize, but some people have had an easier row to hoe, as my grandmother would say, and so maybe when they get to a rocky part in the row, they do not know how to handle it, they do not know where to turn. They haven't built that strength.

Tasha added that being white and male affords them opportunities that predispose them to an attitude of entitlement. She was alluding to institutionalized practices that favor white men, and social-science literature concurs with her point. For example, Feagin refers to Tasha's point as unjust enrichment,[29] which he defines as circumstances that give rise to the obligation of restitution—that is, the receipt and retention of property, money, and benefits that legally and ethically belong to others. He argues that unjust enrichment dates back to before slavery and is now embedded in every aspect of US society.

Kelly, a divorced mother of four, deliberated on how difficult things have been for her, yet she candidly admits she still lacks understanding as to how white men can take their lives. In sharing her views of white men's suicide rate, she too hypothesized that white men haven't been through enough:

> I believe black women deep down inside have a lot more faith and they really believe things are going to get better. They've been through things back in the past with slavery. So, they feel like they can make it through. They feel like they've seen worse, and they can make it through anything. And as far as white men, I really don't know. I don't think that they've been through

enough and they don't know how to take pressure. As a culture, they don't know how to take any oppression because they've been given so much.

The perceptions of Justine, Tasha, Tina, and Kelly regarding the suicidal behavior of white males is in complete contrast to the women's perceptions of their own behavior. Narratives revealed that these women perceive themselves to be strong and white men to be weak. They theorized that their upbringings and experiences with long-term suffering play a critical role in historical and current-day suicide probability. In summary, Figure 5.3 provides a visual illustration of black women's perspectives of white males' suicide rate.

The narratives suggest that black women's perception of white males' weakness is a direct consequence of their perceived notions of white privilege and inability to cope with long-term exposure to stress.

## Summary

A critical analysis of black women's notions of strength and weakness as they relate to the black-white suicide paradox reveals how interviewees define themselves in contrast to white males. Accordingly, black women

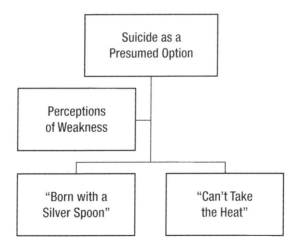

**Figure 5.3 Themes associated with black women's perceptions of white men's rates of suicide.**

depict suicide as the presumed option for those unable to cope with the challenges that life brings, particularly white males. Thus, black women attempt to define themselves in opposition to their conceptions of weak white men, thereby making suicide even less of an option despite their circumstances. Many of the women acknowledged that societal expectations of white men to be "the best" may add to the pressures of these men's daily lives; nonetheless, the women conveyed to me that these negative occurrences could not rival those of the everyday black woman. As Kelly declared, "They don't know how to take any oppression because they've been given so much." This belief was confirmed by Kyndall, who stated, "I don't think they have the tools it takes to survive."

The data revealed that black women see themselves as strong and resilient, and view suicide as an inability to cope. In lieu of literature that often depicts black women as superwomen, interviewees define their "strength" as an intense desire to survive the challenges before them. It is important to note that the women don't necessarily see themselves as having been born strong. Instead they believe their strength developed as a result of having to endure centuries of prejudice and discrimination and their present-day social positions as a result of their race and gender, along with their ability to improvise and get creative when needed.

CHAPTER 6
CONCLUSION
WHAT WE'VE LEARNED FROM BLACK WOMEN
ABOUT THE SUICIDE PARADOX

*What is it like to be a black person in white America today? One step from suicide! What I'm saying is—the psychological warfare games that we have to play every day just to survive. We have to be one way in our communities and one way in the workplace or in the business sector. We can never be ourselves all around. I think that may be a given for all people, but for us particularly; it's really a mental-health problem. It's a wonder we haven't all gone out and killed somebody or killed ourselves.*[1]

### Despite Black Women's Disadvantaged Status

This study of the black-white suicide paradox attempts to elucidate African Americans' infrequent use of suicide to resolve their problems, despite the challenges they face in a racist and sexist society. The findings in this study were central to addressing the following research questions: (1) Why have black women's suicide rates remained consistently low despite the countless social ills that they face? (2) What insight can

African American women provide on the suicide paradox by way of their perceptions of black female and white male rate disparities? (3) What strategies are employed by African American women, either consciously or unconsciously, to elude suicide?

We have established thus far that contemporary black women disproportionately face a number of challenges.[2] Their accounts reveal the difficulties that they face in their attempts to navigate various social settings. As we saw in Chapter 2, the lives of black women can be incredibly complex. Nearly all of my respondents reported having recently encountered discrimination at the hands of whites. This chapter's opening quote is from an accomplished black woman. She is an entrepreneur who has achieved great financial success. Yet despite the fact that she has attained what most would consider the American Dream, she illustrates that financial freedom does little to alleviate the stressors that come with living in a racist, sexist society.

Billionaire media mogul Oprah Winfrey affirmed this point after she encountered racism during a 2013 visit to Switzerland. A store clerk in Zurich declined Winfrey's request to see a $38,000 handbag. According to Winfrey, the clerk stated, "No, no, no, you don't want to see that one. You want to see this one. Because that one will cost too much; you will not be able to afford that."[3] Although Swiss tourism officials later apologized to Winfrey, the damage had already been done. Millions of black girls and women across the globe received a glaring message: individual achievements, such as educational attainment, financial success, or even celebrity status, may do little to combat widespread racial and gender stereotypes.

## Why Study a Low Rate of Suicide?

*Most times when we find out that researchers are going to be studying some facet of black women we cringe. Especially since as of late those studies have revolved around two things—why are we all overweight and why are we all single. Yeah, we're over it. But a new Veterans Affairs study is actually looking to examine something that black women are doing right in order to help other ethnic groups who aren't faring so well. Amazing, right?*[4]

Social scientists have long established the paradoxical relationship between black women's disadvantaged status and their infrequent use of suicide as a solution to their problems.[5] Suicide among nonwhites remains understudied because completed suicides disproportionately occur among the white population. The purpose of this study, then, was to examine black women's perspectives on suicide. In doing so, my intent was to gain a better understanding of black women's narratives about the suicide paradox, to capture a personal take on some of the stressors in black women's lives, and to begin to understand why, despite these stressors, the suicide rate of black women has been so low.

Journalist Alissa Henry's quote at the start of this section references her response to wider audiences taking note of black women's low rate of suicide. Her excitement about researchers taking note of something positive that black women are doing mirrored my participants' responses to my study. During the recruitment phase of the project, I made calls to several venues seeking participants for my study. Within one hour of the first call I received responses from more than half of the study participants. They reported that my study seemed to be one of few that highlighted something black women were doing right. They jumped at the opportunity to promote black women's resiliency despite the individual and structural challenges they face.

## Implications

The findings conveyed in preceding chapters have implications for future empirical research. My original study sought not only to uncover reasons for the black-white suicide paradox, but also to explore black women's protective factors, with the intention of gaining a deeper understanding of their stance regarding this paradoxical phenomenon. This text provides substantive information for suicide-prevention and -intervention scholars. Clinicians who operate community-based mental-health programs and suicide-intervention programs that serve high-risk black women can directly implement the knowledge gained.

### Daily Stressors of Black Women

The study indicated that the participants clearly understood the intricate details of their stressors, and of which coping strategies worked for them. They traced the origins of their stress to their own households as well as to the larger society. Despite this, most intriguing was that the vast majority of the women asserted they had the capability to withstand these challenging circumstances. By doing so they were fulfilling their responsibilities as black women.

One conclusion is that the black women's position on dealing with stressful events is one of self-defined resiliency.[6] What is important here, then, is not so much the stressors that black women endure, but rather their perceptions of the stress and how they see themselves relative to it. They have come to define themselves as resilient survivors with a sense of purpose, which has the effect of insulating them from suicide. For these women, throwing in the towel simply is not an option.

### I Just Want the Pain to End

An additional discovery from this study is related to black women's suicidal ideations. Eleven of the thirty-three black women interviewed had experienced suicidal thoughts, and two of the women had attempted suicide. Thoughts of suicide generally fell into two categories. Some thoughts occurred on a casual basis, and the participants perceived their thoughts to be fairly common given the circumstances. As one woman specifically stated, "Everyone has suicidal thoughts at one time or another." The women appeared to have a clear understanding that their circumstances were fairly extreme, and assumed challenges of this magnitude would most likely evoke suicidal thoughts in anyone under those conditions.

Others considered their thoughts of suicide to be symbolic of an impending disaster. In one instance, a respondent struggled alone with her thoughts for nearly a year before sharing them with a coworker, who ultimately assisted her in getting help. From their accounts I concluded that despite the stressors or underlying triggers for the thoughts, *all* the women perceived a failure to act on suicidal thoughts to be directly attributed to black women's desire to push past their challenging circumstances.

## *Black Women's Perceptions Regarding Their Low Suicide Rate*

Black women's perceptions about their low rate of suicide can be categorized into four themes: (1) notions of managing long-term struggle; (2) notions of how they developed resiliency and strength; (3) use of family or/and social networks; and (4) notions of faith. These themes seem to play a significant role in why black women envision suicide as an unacceptable option.

### WE COME FROM A STRUGGLE

The study participants' narratives revealed that they commonly referenced the trials and tribulations of others as a gauge to cope with their current situations. I title this notion a "sense of long-suffering." They were well aware of the maltreatment that their ancestors faced in this country. They often made claims that present-day African Americans benefit from the endurance established in their bloodline several generations back, and attributed this endurance of suffering as vital in explaining black women's low rate of suicide.

Congruent with this theme, women perceived both historical and current struggles against racial and gendered oppression to be the primary factors in deterring suicidal behavior among current-day black women. Respondents frequently found inspiration and strength in the stories of other African Americans. As we saw in Chapter 5, Tina stated,

> I am of black descent, African American descent. We come in with a struggle. We're pretty much born or the majority of us are born into this cycle of struggle. So when we're faced with adversity, I think it has become part of our nature as well as our DNA, to fight back a little longer, a little harder. You can't miss anything you've never had. The majority of us haven't had that kind of life. So when we don't get it, it's not a big deal, but to have had it and lost it, that's a whole different ball game.

Tina's point was mirrored many other times in my study. An overwhelming majority of the women believed that giving up was not an option, particularly when hardships were held up for comparison to what other African Americans have overcome. For example, some would make statements such as, "If my ancestors survived the injustices of slavery, then

I can certainly survive losing my house or my job." There was a sense among respondents that giving up, which they often equated with suicidal tendencies, was simply an unacceptable option for a black woman. Consequently, though they admit that they face "real" challenges, these challenges are minimal when compared to those their ancestors had to endure. Although some studies have cited cultural differences as a reason for the low rate of suicide among black women,[7] few studies have discussed the notion of black women's resiliency as something that stems from their lineage.

### Seeing Ourselves as Strong and Resilient

Building on their perceptions that the African American cultural experience arose from a struggle, the women in the study also credited their survival to their strength and ability to overcome any situation with which they are presented. The narratives revealed that black women have come to the realization that surviving their struggles takes great ability, an ability not possessed by whites. For instance, these women have found creative ways to cope with an array of challenges—among them, racism and sexism on a regular basis, physical and sexual abuse, catastrophes such as Hurricane Katrina, physical paralysis, and even strokes. Yet the respondents believe that black women are survivors.

Discussions of strength were far from arrogant or boastful, but rather revealed the women's vulnerability. The women took time to place their stories in context. Rather than citing an endless list of things that their "declaration of strength" has brought them through, they revealed pain and disappointment. Within this context, their illustrations of overcoming were more about their desires to not give up rather than proving that they have "superhuman strength." They took great pride in this. Consequently, it was this philosophy that neutralized the notion of suicide. To illustrate, I refer back to Hilldreth's point in Chapter 5:

> Black women's suicide rates are low because as black women, we have become accustomed to being oppressed; it dates back to slavery. We were oppressed for a very, very long time, so we know how to handle stress. We know how to handle things that come our way. . . . If we lose our jobs or if someone hurts us in any way, we know how to handle that because we have been accustomed to getting the short end of the stick

for so many years. So when you are used to living that kind of life, what could make us kill ourselves?

That quote is indicative of many black women's belief that suicide is the easy way out. Along these lines, they defined suicide as an act most often entertained by oppressors (i.e., whites), and as the option that a person is most likely to take when or if he or she has little experience with pain or disappointment. Ultimately, weak was the opposite of the way black women perceived themselves.

### NOTIONS OF FAMILY

As alluded to in Chapter 1, previous studies led me to believe that black women would likely attribute social networks and faith-based beliefs as significant factors in decreasing the likelihood of suicidal behavior among black women. Indeed, both were relevant, with social networks being mentioned slightly more frequently than faith-based beliefs. Social networks, which pertain to social integration, have been understood to be important since Émile Durkheim's pioneering work on suicide, and have been shown to be important in subsequent studies.[8]

Concerning studies specifically examining African Americans, Yanick St. Jean and Joe Feagin speculated that the strength of the black family could play a role in the notably low suicide rates of black women.[9] Additionally, others have argued that the underlying social system of black females needed to be researched further in order to fully understand how familial and kinship ties safeguard against suicidal behaviors of African American women.[10]

How exactly do black women's social networks lower the likelihood that they will commit suicide? Black women identify their connectedness with people in their networks as indispensable. There is a fundamental and unwavering sense of devotion of these women to their family and friends. They frequently made statements such as, "I couldn't kill myself because my family needs me" and "I have committed to helping them, so leaving them is not an option." Therefore, a strong sense of obligation for the well-being of family and friends becomes an essential factor in sustaining low rates of suicide among black women.

Equally important, the black women's narratives exposed the reciprocal effect of the role of others in suppressing suicidal behaviors. The women revealed that members of their networks were equally devoted to them. Thus, they believed that friends and family were no more likely to abandon them than they were to leave friends and family. This made a significant difference because the women felt that they were part of a mutually beneficial relationship.

### NOTIONS OF FAITH

Previous suicide literature concluded that religion encourages social integration, thereby decreasing the likelihood of suicide.[11] The narratives in my study yielded a similar finding. More specifically, the women perceived religious beliefs to function in three ways relative to reducing rates of suicide among black women: (1) religious upbringing, (2) suicide as a sinful act, and (3) seeking God's purpose for one's life. With reference to their religious upbringing, most of the women stated that many of the religious principles that they lived by were instilled in them as young children. We saw this in Clare's point from Chapter 3. Clare is a self-declared atheist, yet you can see remnants of her Christian upbringing in her statement:

> I am very much the result of how I was raised and how I was socialized within the Catholic Church. I was raised to believe that suicide is considered an absolute no-no. There is an overwhelming commitment of African Americans, and in particular African American women, to religion, Christianity. In fact, if you kill yourself you're out of luck all the way around.

Although Clare acknowledged that she does not believe in a higher power, she admits that even at the age of seventy-two, her beliefs about suicide stem from her religious upbringing. Many of the women believed that the religion-based messages taught to them as children helped frame their views on various social issues, and unmistakably so concerning suicide.

Because suicide is defined as a sinful act in Christianity, suicide was something to be avoided. This was also illustrated in Chapter 3, by Delilah:

> Most of the times, the comment is, we [black women] don't do that [commit suicide]. We don't think about taking our own lives, and that is just not something that is common. We think that that's a no-no. And I think spiritually, we're taught that it's a sin. That is what kind of stays in

your head because we were told that you're forgiven for everything but self-murder, which is suicide. So I think that could be one of the things that we kind of hold on to. You don't want to do that. If you take your own life, you're doomed.

In sum, black women's religious upbringing, coupled with the fact that many of the respondents admitted to willfully seeking their life's purpose (i.e., God's plan for them), resulted in black women deeming acts of suicide as unacceptable.

## Black Women's Perceptions of Their Suicide Rate in Relation to That of White Males

Finally, this study revealed black women's perceptions of white men's high rate of suicide in comparison to their own very low rate. Just as black women defined themselves as strong in relation to their position in society, they perceived white men to be weak. Using this dichotomy, black women characterized their long-term exposure to stressful conditions, coupled with their notions of faith and family, as motivations for their uncompromising strength. They attributed the lack of these same characteristics in white males as causal factors for their high rate of suicide. Participants cited white males' inexperience with long-term stress plus their unjustified privilege (i.e., white privilege) as rationales for their higher rates of suicide. Similar findings by Rheeda Walker, David Lester, and Sean Joe revealed that white men were more likely than blacks to believe they had control over their own lives; blacks overwhelmingly placed their faith in a higher power.[12] These researchers also claimed that the basis for this frame of mind could be traced back to white men's dominant positions in society.

Black women in this study also offered up their perceptions of the causes behind white men's suicide rate. White men know nothing of elemental struggle, they believed, and this resulted in their caving in under pressure. The respondents, therefore, saw suicide by white males as a not-uncommon response to troubling times; additionally, the women commonly stated that white men don't even have to be going through anything substantial to kill themselves or that's just what white men do. For example, in Chapter 5 we have Tasha's bold statement:

> White men have a lot of things that are working for them just by virtue of the fact that they are white and they are males, and so they have more advantages. I hate to generalize, but some people have had an easier row to hoe, as my grandmother would say, and so maybe when they get to a rocky part in the row, they do not know how to handle it, they do not know where to turn. They haven't built that strength.

The primary conclusion that can be drawn here is that black women perceive struggle and survival to be associated with the black experience. In contrast, they perceive both lack of struggle and white privilege to breed weakness and suicidal tendencies. The narratives also revealed that black women perceive suicide as an act of whiteness and thereby of weakness. These perceptions were glaringly negative, and black women used this as an opportunity to define themselves and distance themselves from the thought of suicide.

The suicide paradox is an intriguing area of research. Although the women with whom I spoke had various levels of education and income, and different life experiences, there was surprisingly homogeneity within their responses. This study has revealed that black women's perceptions of themselves through their historical and contemporary struggles, their notions of faith and family, and their self-ascribed labels of strength serve as preventive mechanisms against their committing suicide. Along these same lines, black women have constructed their own meanings of suicide that connect it with weakness and to whiteness. As a result, the act of suicide is intrinsically contrary to the individual definitions that they have developed of themselves.

These findings could prove crucial in understanding the lack of suicide among the African American population more generally, because this project makes linkages to the literature on suicide, race, and gender. Therefore, understanding black women's perceptions of why their suicide rates have remained consistently low is critical to understanding how black women fare in a world where they are just as prone to suicide as white males.

## Future Research

This study's purpose was to contribute to the literature by way of providing rich, detailed information to a relatively unstudied area. As a result, I challenge researchers to continue on the path of providing more detailed data regarding black-white suicide disparities. Qualitative approaches to this topic can be one way to truly gain insight into the phenomenon.

I encourage researchers to further explore a preliminary finding of this study, concerning moments of crisis. These are points in time when black women had suicidal thoughts but decided against an attempt or the act itself. A substantial number of the women interviewed reported contemplating suicide, but of the nine who did, only one attempt was reported. It would be interesting to study this phenomenon further with the hope of gaining insight into these as-yet-unexplored occurrences.

Finally, this study, along with others, has found that social networks appear to play a significant role in black women's perceptions of suicide. It would, then, be particularly interesting to explore changes (if any) in suicide perceptions among African American women who have experienced disruptions in their social networks. Groups of interest, for example, would be incarcerated African American women and victims of Hurricane Katrina.

# Notes

## Foreword

1. Myrdal, Gunnar, *An American Dilemma,* vol. 2 (New York: McGraw-Hill, 1964), pp. 928–929.
2. Ellison, Ralph, *Shadow and Act* (New York: Random House, 1995), pp. 315–316. Italics added.
3. Moynihan, Daniel P., *The Negro Family: the Case for National Action* (Washington, DC: US Government Printing Office, 1965), p. 5.

## Chapter 1

1. Jedlicka, Davor, Yongsock Shin, and Everett S. Lee, "Suicide among Blacks," *Phylon (1960–)* 38 (1977): 448–455 (quote, p. 448).
2. Griffin-Fennell, Felicia, and Michelle Williams, "Examining the Complexities of Suicidal Behavior in the African American Community," *Journal of Black Psychology* 32 (2006): 303–319; Lester, David, *Suicide in African Americans* (Commack, NY: Nova Science Publishers, 1998); Stack, Steven, and Ira Wasserman, "The Effect of Marriage, Family, and Religious Ties on African American Suicide Ideology," *Journal of Marriage and the Family* 57 (1995): 215–222.
3. Barnes, Donna, and Carl C. Bell, "Paradoxes of Black Suicide," *National Journal* 20 (2003): 2–4; Kirk, Alton R., and Donna Holland Barnes, *Black Suicide: The Tragic Reality of America's Deadliest Secret* (Silver Springs, MD: Beckham Publications, 2009); Lester, *Suicide in African Americans*; Rockett, Ian, Julie

Samora, and Jeffrey Coben, "The Black-White Suicide Paradox: Possible Effects of Misclassification," *Social Science and Medicine* 63 (2006): 2165–2175.

4. Centers for Disease Control and Prevention (CDC), "1950–2006, United States Suicide Injury Deaths and Rates per 100,000," Web-based Injury Statistics Query and Reporting Sytem (WISQARS), April 2007, www.cdc.gov/injury/wisqars/index.html (accessed June 4, 2008).

5. Hendin, Herbert, *Black Suicide* (New York: Basic Books, 1969); Lester, *Suicide in African Americans*; Alvin F. Poussaint, *Lay My Burden Down: Suicide and the Mental Health Crisis among African-Americans* (Boston: Beacon Press, 2001).

6. McIntosh, John, *U.S.A. Suicide 2004 Official Final Data* (Washington, DC: American Association of Suicidology, 2004).

7. US Census Bureau, "Educational Attainment of the Population 15 Years and Over, by Age, Sex, Race and Hispanic Origin" (Washington, DC: US Census Bureau, 2000).

8. "African American Suicide Fact Sheet," American Association of Suicidology, 2006, http://www.suicidology.org/c/document_library/get_file?folderId=232&name=DLFE-20.pdf (accessed June 12, 2010).

9. CDC, "1950–2006, United States Suicide Injury Deaths and Rates per 100,000."

10. CDC, "1950–2006, United States Suicide Injury Deaths and Rates per 100,000."

11. Garlow, Steven J., David Purselle, and Michael Heninger, "Ethnic Differences in Patterns of Suicide across the Life Cycle," *American Journal of Psychiatry* 162 (2005): 319–323.

12. Fernquist, Robert M., "Does Single Motherhood Protect against Black Female Suicide?," *Archives of Suicide Research* 8 (2004): 163–171.

13. CDC, "1950–2006, United States Suicide Injury Deaths and Rates per 100,000."

14. Office of Statistics and Programming and National Center for Injury Prevention, "2008 Self-Harm All Injury Causes Nonfatal Injuries and Rates per 100,000, Ages 18–80," May 2008, http://webappa.cdc.gov/sasweb/ncipc/nfirates2001.html (accessed March 23, 2010).

15. Alston, Maude H., and Sharon Eylar Anderson, "Suicidal Behavior in African American Women," in *Women and Suicidal Behavior,* ed. S. S. Canetto and D. Lester (New York: Springer Publishing Company, 1995), pp. 133–143.

16. Office of Statistics and Programming and National Center for Injury Prevention, "2008 Self-Harm All Injury Causes Nonfatal Injuries and Rates per 100,000, Ages 18–80."

17. Durkheim, Émile, *On Suicide*, trans. Robin Buss (London: Penguin, 2007 [1897]); Lester, *Suicide in African Americans*; Charles Prudhomme, "The Problem of Suicide in the American Negro," *Psychoanalytic Review* 25 (1938): 187–204, 372–391; St. Jean, Yanick, and Joe R. Feagin, *Double Burden: Black Women and Everyday Racism* (New York: M. E. Sharpe, 1998).

18. Beauboeuf-Lafontant, Tamara, "You Have to Show Strength: An Exploration of Gender, Race, and Depression," *Gender and Society* 21 (2007): 28–51; Hill Collins, Patricia, *Black Feminist Thought: Knowledge, Consciousness, and the Politics of Empowerment* (New York: Routledge, 2000); Farrington, Lisa E., "Reinventing Herself: The Black Female Nude," *Women's Art Journal* 24 (2003): 15–23; Gray White, Deborah, *Ar'n't I a Woman? Female Slaves in the Plantation South* (New York: W. W. Norton and Company, 1999); Jones, Charisse, and Kumea Shorter-Gooden, *Shifting: The Double Lives of Black Women in America* (New York: HarperCollins, 2003); Krieger, Nancy, and Mary Bassett, "The Health of Black Folk: Disease, Class, and Ideology in Science," in *The "Racial" Economy of Science toward a Democratic Future*, ed. S. Harding (Indianapolis: Indiana University Press, 1993), pp. 161–169; Lerner, Gerda, *Black Women in White America* (New York: Vintage Books, 1973); Staples, Robert, *The Black Woman in America* (Chicago: Nelson-Hall Publishers, 1973); St. Jean and Feagin, *Double Burden*.

19. Rockett, Samora, and Coben, "The Black-White Suicide Paradox."

20. Office of Minority Health, *Data Statistics* (Washington, DC: US Department of Health and Human Services, 2007); Eberhardt, M. S., D. D. Ingram, and D. M. Makuc, *Urban and Rural Health Chartbook* (Hyattsville, MD: Centers for Disease Control, 2001).

21. Weigers, Margaret E., and Susan K. Drilea, *Research Findings #10: Health Status and Limitations: A Comparison of Hispanics, Blacks, and Whites, 1996* (Rockville, MD: Agency for Healthcare Research and Quality, 1999).

22. Eberhardt, Ingram, and Makuc, *Urban and Rural Health Chartbook*.

23. Grason, Holly, Cynthia Minkovitz, Dawn Misra, and Donna Strobino, "Women's Health Data Book: A Profile of Women's Health in the United States," in *Impact of Social and Economic Factors on Women's Health*, ed. D. Misra (Washington, DC: Jacobs Institute of Women's Health and The Henry J. Kaiser Family Foundation, 2001), pp. 2–13.

24. Brewer, Rose H., "Black Women in Poverty: Some Comments on Female-Headed Families," *Signs* 13 (1988): 331–339.

25. Bell, Derrick, *And We Are Not Saved* (New York: Basic Books, 1987).

26. Staples, Robert, "Social Structure and Black Family Life: An Analysis of Current Trends," *Journal of Black Studies* 17 (1987): 267–286.

27. US Census Bureau, "Educational Attainment of the Population 25 Years and Over, by Age, Sex, Race, and Hispanic Origin" (Washington, DC: US Census Bureau, 2013).

28. US Census Bureau, "Educational Attainment in the United States: 2007" (Washington, DC: American Community Survey, 2009).

29. Barbee, Evelyn L., "African American Women and Depression: A Review and Critique of the Literature," *Archives of Psychiatric Nursing* 6 (1992): 257–265; Suicide Prevention Resource Center, "Suicide among Black Americans," 2010, www.sprc.org/library/ai.an.facts.pdf (accessed June 27, 2010).

30. Jones and Shorter-Gooden, *Shifting*.

31. Moorer, Talise D., "Stress More Crippling in Black Women Than White Counterparts," *New York Amsterdam News* 97 (2006): 32–43.

32. Feagin, Joe R., *Systemic Racism* (New York: Routledge, 2006).

33. Mindel, Charles H., Robert W. Habenstein, and Roosevelt Wright Jr., *Ethnic Families in America: Patterns and Variations* (Upper Saddle River, NJ: Prentice Hall, 1998).

34. Takaki, Ronald, *A Different Mirror: A History of Multicultural America* (Boston, MA: Little, Brown and Company, 1993).

35. Gerstle, Gary, *American Crucible: Race and Nation in the Twentieth Century* (Princeton, NJ: Princeton University Press, 2001); US Congress, "The Reconstruction Act," in *The African-American Archive*, vol. 16, ed. K. Wright (New York: Black Dog and Leventhal Publishers, 2009), pp. 391–393.

36. Feagin, Joe R., *Racist America* (New York: Routledge, 2001).

37. Feagin, *Racist America*.

38. Jones, Lani, "Enhancing Psychosocial Competence among Black Women in College," *Social Work* 49 (2004): 75–83.

39. Bhugra, Dinesh, and Oyedeji Ayonrinde, "Racism, Racial Life Events and Mental Ill Health," *Advances in Psychiatric Treatment* 7 (2001): 343–349.

40. Feagin, Joe R., and Melvin Sikes, *Living with Racism: The Black Middle-Class Experience* (Boston: Beacon Press, 1995); Feagin, *Racist America*.

41. Collins, *Black Feminist Thought*; West, Traci C., *Wounds of the Spirit: Black Women, Violence, and Resistance Ethics* (New York: New York University Press, 1999).

42. Gray White, *Ar'n't I a Woman?*; Neville, Helen A., and Jennifer Hamer, "We Make Freedom: An Exploration of Revolutionary Black Feminism," *Journal of Black Studies* 31 (2001): 437–461; Witt, Doris, "How Mama Started to Get Large: Black Eating Disorders, Fetal Rights, and Black Female Appetite," in *Black Hunger: Food and the Politics of US Identity* (New York: Oxford University Press, 1999), pp. 183–199.

43. Beauboeuf-Lafontant, Tamara, "Listening Past the Lies That Make Us Sick: A Voice-Centered Analysis of Strength and Depression among Black Women," *Qualitative Sociology* 31 (2008): 391–406; Bhugra and Ayonrinde, "Racism, Racial Life Events and Mental Ill Health"; Moorer, "Stress More Crippling in Black Women Than White Counterparts"; Shapiro, Thomas M., *The Hidden Cost of Being African American: How Wealth Perpetuates Inequality* (New York: Oxford University Press, 2004); St. Jean and Feagin, *Double Burden*; Staples, *The Black Woman in America*.

44. Brown, Delindus R., and Wanda F. Anderson, "A Survey of the Black Woman and the Persuasion Process: The Study of Strategies of Identification and Resistance," *Journal of Black Studies* 9 (1978): 233–248; Shorter-Gooden, Kumea, "Multiple Resistance Strategies: How African American Women Cope with Racism and Sexism," *Journal of Black Psychology* 30 (2004): 406–425; West, *Wounds of the Spirit*.

45. Jones and Shorter-Gooden, *Shifting*; Sands, Aimee, "Never Meant to Survive, a Black Woman's Journey: An Interview with Evelyn Hammonds," in *Women, Science, and Technology: A Reader in the Feminist Science Studies*, ed. Mary Wyer, Donna Geisman, Hatice Orun Ozturk, and Marta Wayne (New York: Routledge, 2001), pp. 5–38.

46. Durkheim, *On Suicide*.

47. Durkheim, *On Suicide*; Fernquist, Robert M., "Education, Race/Ethnicity, Age, Sex, and Suicide: Individual-Level Data in the United States, 1991–1994," *Current Research in Social Psychology* 6 (2001): 277–291; Lester, *Suicide in African Americans*; Neeleman, Jan, Simon Wessely, and Glyn Lewis, "Suicide Acceptability in African and White Americans: The Role of Religion," *Journal of Nervous and Mental Disease* 186 (1998): 12–16; Nisbet, Paul A., "Protective Factors for Suicidal Black Females," *Suicide and Life-Threatening Behavior* 26 (1996): 325–341; Walker, Rheeda L., David Lester, and Sean Joe, "Lay Theories of Suicide: An Examination of Culturally Relevant Suicide Beliefs and Attributions among African Americans and European Americans," *Journal of Black Psychology* 32 (2006): 320–334.

48. Durkheim, *On Suicide*; Lester, *Suicide in African Americans*; Stack and Wasserman, "The Effect of Marriage, Family, and Religious Ties."

49. Goodwin, Paula Y., William D. Mosher, and Anjani Chandra, "Marriage and Cohabitation in the United States: A Statistical Portrait Based on Cycle 6 (2002) of the National Survey of Family Growth," vol. 23 (Hyattsville, MD: US Department of Health and Human Services, 2010).

50. Bearman, Peter S., "The Social Structure of Suicide," *Sociological Forum* 6 (1991): 501.

51. Girard, Chris, "Age, Gender, and Suicide: A Cross-National Analysis," *American Sociological Review* 58 (1993): 553–574.
52. Girard, "Age, Gender, and Suicide."
53. Prudhomme, "The Problem of Suicide in the American Negro."
54. Prudhomme, "The Problem of Suicide in the American Negro."
55. Hendin, *Black Suicide*.
56. Hendin, *Black Suicide*.
57. Barnes and Bell, "Paradoxes of Black Suicide"; Lester, *Suicide in African Americans*; Taylor-Gibbs, Jewelle, "African American Suicide: A Cultural Paradox," *Suicide and Life-Threatening Behavior* 27 (1997): 68–79.
58. Jedlicka, Shin, and Lee, "Suicide among Blacks."
59. Jones and Shorter-Gooden, *Shifting*.
60. Collins, *Black Feminist Thought*; Gray White, *Ar'n't I a Woman?*
61. Nora, Pierre, "Between Memory and History: Les Lieux de Mémoire," *Representations* 26 (1989): 7–24.
62. Burawoy, Michael, "The Extended Case Method," in *Ethnography Unbound: Power and Resistance in the Modern Metropolis,* ed. M. Burawoy, A. Burton, A. A. Ferguson, K. J. Fox, J. Hurst, C. Kurzman, L. Salzinger, J. Schiffman, and S. Ui (Berkeley: University of California Press, 1991).
63. Burawoy, "The Extended Case Method," p. x.
64. West, *Wounds of the Spirit*.
65. Fernquist, "Education, Race/Ethnicity, Age, Sex, and Suicide"; Stephens, B. Joyce, "The Pseudosuicidal Female: A Cautionary Tale," in *Women and Suicidal Behavior,* ed. S. S. Canetto and D. Lester (New York: Springer Publishing Company, 1995).
66. Strauss, Anselm, and Juliet M. Corbin, *Basics of Qualitative Research: Techniques and Procedures for Developing Grounded Theory* (Thousands Oaks, CA: Sage Publications, 1998).
67. Demos, Vasilikie, "Black Family Studies in the Journal of Marriage and the Family and the Issue of Distortion: A Trend Analysis," *Journal of Marriage and the Family* 52 (1990): 603–612; Rainwater, Lee, and William L. Yancey, *The Moynihan Report and the Politics of Controversy* (Cambridge and London: MIT Press, 1967).
68. Dyson, Michael, "Do You Believe That Black Women Have Too Much Attitude?," *Essence* 37 (2006): 127; Jones and Shorter-Gooden, *Shifting*; St. Jean and Feagin, *Double Burden*.
69. Lugo, Luis, Sandra Stencel, John Green, Gregory Smith, Dan Cox, Allison Pond, Tracy Miller, Elizabeth Podrebarac, and Michelle Ralston, "U.S. Religious Landscape Survey" (Washington, DC: Pew Forum on Religion and Public Life, 2008).

## Chapter 2

1. In this quote, Jennifer, a participant in the study, responds to an open-ended question that asked her about stressors facing contemporary black women.

2. Griffin-Fennell, Felicia, and Michelle Williams, "Examining the Complexities of Suicidal Behavior in the African American Community," *Journal of Black Psychology* 32 (2006): 303–319.

3. Aguirre, Adalberto, and Jonathan H. Turner, *American Ethnicity: The Dynamics and Consequences of Discrimination* (New York: McGraw-Hill Higher Education, 2001).

4. Beauboeuf-Lafontant, Tamara, "You Have to Show Strength: An Exploration of Gender, Race, and Depression," *Gender and Society* 21 (2007): 28–51; Collins, Patricia Hill, *Black Feminist Thought: Knowledge, Consciousness, and the Politics of Empowerment* (New York: Routledge, 2000); Farrington, Lisa E., "Reinventing Herself: The Black Female Nude," *Women's Art Journal* 24 (2003): 15–23; Gray White, Deborah, *Ar'n't I a Woman? Female Slaves in the Plantation South* (New York: W. W. Norton and Company, 1999); Jones, Charisse, and Kumea Shorter-Gooden, *Shifting: The Double Lives of Black Women in America* (New York: HarperCollins, 2003); Krieger, Nancy, and Mary Bassett, "The Health of Black Folk: Disease, Class, and Ideology in Science," in *The "Racial" Economy of Science toward a Democratic Future,* ed. S. Harding (Indianapolis: Indiana University Press, 1993), pp. 161–169; Lerner, Gerda, *Black Women in White America* (New York: Vintage Books, 1973); St. Jean, Yanick, and Joe R. Feagin, *Double Burden: Black Women and Everyday Racism* (New York: M. E. Sharpe, 1998); Staples, Robert, *The Black Woman in America* (Chicago: Nelson-Hall Publishers, 1973).

5. Center to Reduce Cancer Health Disparities, "Health Disparities Defined" (Rockville, MD: National Cancer Institute, 2007), http://crchd.cancer.gov/ (accessed September 16, 2008).

6. US Census Bureau, "Income, Poverty, and Health Insurance Coverage in the United States: 2012—Report and Detailed Tables," http://www.census.gov/hhes/www/poverty/data/incpovhlth/2012/index.html (accessed September 23, 2013).

7. Bell, Derrick, *And We Are Not Saved* (New York: Basic Books, 1987); Brewer, Rose H., "Black Women in Poverty: Some Comments on Female-Headed Families," *Signs* 13 (1988): 331–339; Furstenberg, Frank F., "The Making of the Black Family: Race and Class in Qualitative Studies in the Twentieth Century," *Annual Review of Sociology* 33 (2007): 429–448.

8. US Census Bureau, "Income, Poverty, and Health Insurance Coverage."

9. DeNavas-Walt, Carmen, Bernadette D. Proctor, and Cheryl Hill Lee, "Income, Poverty, and Health Insurance Coverage in the United States: 2012," *Current Population Reports,* US Census Bureau (Washington, DC: Government Printing Office, 2013).

10. Darity, William, and Samuel L. Myers, "Does Welfare Dependency Cause Female Headship? The Case of the Black Family," *Journal of Marriage and Family* 46 (1984): 779; DeNavas-Walt, Proctor, and Lee, "Income, Poverty, and Health Insurance Coverage."

11. Hill, R. B., *The Strengths of African American Families: Twenty-Five Years Later* (Lanham, MD: University Press of America, 1999); Kendel, Denise B., "Race, Maternal, and Adolescent Aspiration," *American Journal of Sociology* 76 (1971): 999–1020.

12. Allen, Walter R., "The Social and Economic Statuses of Black Women in the United States," *Phylon* 42 (1981): 26–40.

13. Brewer, "Black Women in Poverty."

14. Fussman, Chris, Violanda Grigorescu, Steve Korzeniewski, Sarah Lyon Callo, Bridget Protas, and Ann Rafferty, "Women's Health Brief: Depression Life Span Approach," Michigan Department of Community Health, 2007.

15. Beauboeuf-Lafontant, "You Have to Show Strength"; Belle, Deborah, and Joanne Doucet, "Poverty, Inequality, and Discrimination as Sources of Depression among U.S. Women," *Psychology of Women Quarterly* 27 (2003): 101–113; Jones and Shorter-Gooden, *Shifting.*

16. St. Jean and Feagin, *Double Burden;* Myrdal, Gunnar, *An American Dilemma: The Negro Problem and Modern Democracy* (New York: Harper and Row, 1969); Staples, *The Black Woman in America.*

17. Arias, Elizabeth, Robert N. Anderson, Hsiang-Ching Kung, Sherry L. Murphy, and Kenneth D. Kochanek, "Deaths: Final Data for 2001," *National Vital Statistics Reports* 52 (2003): 1–116; Ferraro, Kenneth F., and Melissa M. Farmer, "Double Jeopardy, Aging as Leveler, or Persistent Health Inequality? A Longitudinal Analysis of White and Black Americans," *Journals of Gerontology* 51B (1996): S319–S328.

18. Kung, H. C., X. Liu, and S. Juon, "Risk Factors for Suicide in Caucasians and in African Americans: A Matched Case-Control Study," *Social Psychiatry* 33 (1998): 155–161.

19. Lester, David, *Suicide in African Americans* (Commack, NY: Nova Science Publishers, 1998); Taylor-Gibbs, Jewelle, "African American Suicide: A Cultural Paradox," *Suicide and Life-Threatening Behavior* 27 (1997): 68–79; Utsey,

Shawn O., Joshua N. Hook, and Pia Stanard, "A Re-Examination of Cultural Factors That Mitigate Risk and Promote Resilience in Relation to African American Suicide: A Review of the Literature and Recommendations for Future Research," *Death Studies* 31 (2007): 399–416.

20. Lumumba-Kasongo, Mana, "My Black Skin Makes My White Coat Vanish," in *Race, Class, and Gender in the United States,* ed. P. S. Rothenberg (New York: Worth Publishers, 2007).

21. Jones and Shorter-Gooden, *Shifting*.

22. Jones and Shorter-Gooden, *Shifting*, p. 7.

23. Feagin, Joe R., and Melvin Sikes, *Living with Racism: The Black Middle-Class Experience* (Boston: Beacon Press, 1995).

24. Gallagher, Charles A., "The Social and Political Functions of Erasing the Color Line in Post Race America," in *Rethinking the Color Line: Readings in Race and Ethnicity,* 4th ed., C. A. Gallagher (New York: McGraw-Hill, 2009), p. 100.

25. Welter, Barbra, "The Cult of True Womanhood: 1820–1860," *American Quarterly* 18 (1966): 151–174.

26. Collins, *Black Feminist Thought*.

27. Townsend-Gilkes, Cheryl, *If It Wasn't for the Women . . . : Black Women's Experience and Womanist Culture in Church and Community* (Maryknoll, NY: Orbis Books, 2001).

28. Muhammad, Shaida, "Superwoman Syndrome: Are Black Women Killing Themselves to Be Strong?," *Ebony* (2012), http://www.ebony.com/wellness-empowerment/superwoman-syndrome/2#axzz2nm2ZDbfx (accessed Februrary 19, 2013).

29. Thompson, Krissah, "Survey Paints Portrait of Black Women in America," *Washington Post,* January 22, 2012, http://www.washingtonpost.com/politics/survey-paints-portrait-of-black-women-in-america/2011/12/22/gIQAvxFcJQ_story.html (accessed March 3, 2013).

30. Norris, Claire M., and Flint D. Mitchell, "Exploring the Stress-Support-Distress Process among Black Women," *Journal of Black Studies* 45 (2014): 3–18.

31. Goldsmith, Sarah K., "Suicide Prevention and Intervention: Summary of a Workshop," (workshop held at Institute of Medicine, Washington, DC: National Academy Press, 2001).

32. Crosby, Alex E., LaVonne Ortega, and Cindi Melanson, "Self-Directed Violence Surveillance: Uniform Definitions and Recommended Data Elements," Version 1.0 (Atlanta: Centers for Disease Control and Prevention, 2011).

## Chapter 3

1. In this quote, Kyndall, a respondent in the study, initially conveyed that black women's faith is responsible for their low rate of suicide. She then elaborated on the role that faith plays in curtailing suicidal behavior among black women.

2. Lane, Derrick, "Singer Vivian Green Finds Healing in Faith" (2013), http://blackdoctor.org/96293/vivian-green-suicide/2/ (accessed June 12, 2013).

3. Early, Kevin, *Religion and Suicide in the African American Community* (Westport, CT: Greenwood Press, 1992); Mattis, J. S., "Religion and Spirituality in the Meaning-Making and Coping Experiences of African American Women: A Qualitative Analysis," *Psychology of Women Quarterly* 26 (2002): 309–321; Neeleman, Jan, Simon Wessely, and Glyn Lewis, "Suicide Acceptability in African and White Americans: The Role of Religion," *Journal of Nervous and Mental Disease* 186 (1998): 12–16; Stack, Steven, and Ira Wasserman, "The Effect of Marriage, Family, and Religious Ties on African American Suicide Ideology," *Journal of Marriage and the Family* 57 (1995): 215–222; Walker, Rheeda L., David Lester, and Sean Joe, "Lay Theories of Suicide: An Examination of Culturally Relevant Suicide Beliefs and Attributions among African Americans and European Americans," *Journal of Black Psychology* 32 (2006): 320–334.

4. Durkheim, Émile, *On Suicide*, trans. Robin Buss (London: Penguin, 1897); Fernquist, Robert M., "Does Single Motherhood Protect against Black Female Suicide?," *Archives of Suicide Research* 8 (2004): 163–171; Neeleman, Wessely, and Lewis, "Suicide Acceptability in African and White Americans." Nisbet, Paul A., "Protective Factors for Suicidal Black Females," *Suicide and Life-Threatening Behavior* 26 (1996): 325–341; Prudhomme, Charles, "The Problem of Suicide in the American Negro," *Psychoanalytic Review* 25 (1938): 187–204, 372–391; Walker, Lester, and Joe, "Lay Theories of Suicide."

5. Marion, Michelle S., and Lillian M. Range, "African American College Women's Suicide Buffers," *Suicide and Life-Threatening Behavior* 33 (2001): 33–43.

6. Neeleman, Wessely, and Lewis, "Suicide Acceptability in African and White Americans."

7. Early, Kevin, *Religion and Suicide in the African American Community* (Westport, CT: Greenwood Press, 1992); Neeleman, Wessely, and Lewis, "Suicide Acceptability in African and White Americans"; Fernquist, "Does Single Motherhood Protect against Black Female Suicide?," pp. 163–171; Griffin-Fennell, Felicia, and Michelle Williams, "Examining the Complexities of Suicidal Behavior in the African American Community," *Journal of Black Psychology* 32 (2006): 303–319; Stack and Wasserman, "The Effect of Marriage, Family, and Religious Ties on African American Suicide Ideology."

8. Early, Kevin, "'It's a White Thing': An Exploration of Beliefs about Suicide in the African-American Community," *Deviant Behavior* 14 (1993): 277–296.

9. Lugo, Luis, Sandra Stencel, John Green, Gregory Smith, Dan Cox, Allison Pond, Tracy Miller, Elizabeth Podrebarac, and Michelle Ralston, "U.S. Religious Landscape Survey" (Washington, DC: Pew Forum on Religion and Public Life, 2008).

10. Lugo et al., "U.S. Religious Landscape Survey."

11. *Washington Post*, "Washington Post–Kaiser Family Foundation Poll of Black Women in America," http://www.washingtonpost.com/wp-srv/special/nation/black-women-in-america/ (accessed March 8, 2012).

12. Walker, Lester, and Joe, "Lay Theories of Suicide."

13. Early, *Religion and Suicide in the African American Community*; Neeleman, Wessely, and Lewis, "Suicide Acceptability in African and White Americans"; Shorter-Gooden, Kumea, "Multiple Resistance Strategies: How African American Women Cope with Racism and Sexism," *Journal of Black Psychology* 30 (2004): 406–425; Wingate, LaRicka R., Leonardo Bobadilla, Andrea B. Burns, and Kelly C. Cukrowicz, "Suicidality in African American Men: The Roles of Southern Residence, Religiosity, and Social Support," *Suicide and Life-Threatening Behavior* 35 (2005): 615; Royster, Michael D., "Are Things Getting Worse?," *The African American Pulpit* 13, no. 2 (2010): 85–87.

14. Durkheim, *On Suicide*; Neeleman, Wessely, and Lewis, "Suicide Acceptability in African and White Americans."

15. Jakes, T. D., http://christian-quotes.ochristian.com/T.D.-Jakes-Quotes/ (accessed March 8, 2013).

16. Durkheim, *On Suicide*; Neeleman, Wessely, and Lewis, "Suicide Acceptability in African and White Americans"; Walker, Lester, and Joe, "Lay Theories of Suicide."

## Chapter 4

1. In this quote, Clare, a respondent in the study, offers her take on why black women's suicide rate is low.

2. Nisbet, Paul A., "Protective Factors for Suicidal Black Females," *Suicide and Life-Threatening Behavior* 26 (1996): 325–341.

3. Nisbet, "Protective Factors for Suicidal Black Females"; Fernquist, Robert M., "Education, Race/Ethnicity, Age, Sex, and Suicide: Individual-Level Data in the United States, 1991–1994," *Current Research in Social Psychology* 6 (2001): 277–291.

4. Andrews, Edwina Uehara, Jose Morales, and Dolores G. Norton, *The Neighborhood Self Help Project* (Chicago: University of Chicago, School of Social Service Administration, 1980); Caplan, Gerald, *Support Systems and Community Mental Health: Lectures on Concept Development* (New York: Behavioral Publications, 1974); President's Commission on Mental Health, "Report to the President from the President's Commission on Mental Health," vol. 4 (Washington, DC: Government Printing Office, 1978).

5. Cobb, Sidney, "Social Support as a Moderator of Life Stress," *Psychosomatic Medicine* 38 (1976): 300–314; Croog, Sidney, A. Lipson, and Stanley Levine, "Help Patterns in Severe Illness: The Roles of Kin Network, Non-Family Resources and Institutions," *Journal of Marriage and the Family* 34 (1972): 32–41; Turner, R. Jay, "Direct, Indirect, and Moderating Effects of Social Support on Psychological Distress and Associated Conditions," in *Psychosocial Stress: Trends in Theory and Research,* ed. H. B. Kaplan (Orlando: Academic Press, 1983), pp. 105–155; Turner, R. Jay, "Social Support as a Contingency in Psychological Well-Being," *Journal of Health and Social Behavior* 22 (1981): 357–367.

6. Turner, "Social Support as a Contingency in Psychological Well-Being," p. 365.

7. Turner, "Social Support as a Contingency in Psychological Well-Being," pp. 357–367

8. Nisbet, "Protective Factors for Suicidal Black Females."

9. Fraser, Idelle M., Louise-Anne McNutt, Carla Clark, Deborah Williams-Muhammed, and Robin Lee, "Social Support Choices for Help with Abusive Relationships: Perceptions of African American Women," *Journal of Family Violence* 17 (2002): 363–375.

10. Lewis-Harris, Treniece, and Sherry Davis-Molock, "Cultural Orientation, Family Cohesion, and Family Support in Suicide Ideation and Depression among African American College Students," *Suicide and Life-Threatening Behavior* 30 (2000): 341–353.

11. Lewis-Harris and Davis-Molock, "Cultural Orientation, Family Cohesion, and Family Support in Suicide Ideation and Depression"; Nisbet, "Protective Factors for Suicidal Black Females"; Fernquist, Robert M., "Does Single Motherhood Protect against Black Female Suicide?," *Archives of Suicide Research* 8 (2004): 163–171; Goldsmith, Sarah K., "Risk Factors for Suicide: Summary of a Workshop" (Washington, DC: National Academy Press, 2001); Griffin-Fennell, Felicia, and Michelle Williams, "Examining the Complexities of Suicidal Behavior in the African American Community," *Journal of Black Psychology* 32 (2006):

303–319; Prudhomme, Charles, "The Problem of Suicide in the American Negro," *Psychoanalytic Review* 25 (1938): 187–204, 372–391.

12. Durkheim, Émile, *Suicide* (London: Penguin, 1897).

13. Nisbet, "Protective Factors for Suicidal Black Females."

14. Frazier, Edward Franklin, *The Negro Family in the United States* (Chicago: University of Chicago Press, 1939); Rainwater, Lee, and William L. Yancey, *The Moynihan Report and the Politics of Controversy* (Cambridge and London: MIT Press, 1967); Moynihan, Patrick, *The Negro Family: The Case for National Action*, Office of Policy Planning and Research, US Department of Labor (Washington, DC: Howard University, 1965), pp. 1–78.

15. Genovese, Eugene D., "The Myth of the Absent Family," in *The Black Family: Essays and Studies*, ed. R. Staples (Belmont, CA: Wadsworth Publishing Company, 1999), pp. 25–32.

16. Royse, David D., and Gladys T. Turner, "Strengths of Black Families: A Black Community's Perspective," *Social Work* 25 (1980): 407–409; Williams, Sharon E., and Dolores Finger Wright, "Empowerment: The Strengths of Black Families Revisited," *Journal of Multicultural Social Work* 2 (1992): 23–36.

17. Hill, Robert, *The Strengths of Black Families* (New York: Emerson Hall, 1972).

18. Kilpatrick, Allie C., "Future Directions for the Black Family," *Family Coordinator* 28 (1979): 347.

19. Feagin, Joe R., *Racist America* (New York: Routledge, 2001).

20. West, Traci C., *Wounds of the Spirit: Black Women, Violence, and Resistance Ethics* (New York: New York University Press, 1999).

21. West, *Wounds of the Spirit*, p. 42.

22. Sands, Aimee, "Never Meant to Survive, A Black Woman's Journey: An Interview with Evelyn Hammonds," in *Women, Science, and Technology: A Reader in the Feminist Science Studies*, ed. Mary Wyer, Donna Geisman, Hatice Orun Ozturk, Marta Wayne (New York: Routledge, 2001), pp. 5–38.

23. Sands, "Never Meant to Survive, A Black Woman's Journey," p. 25.

24. Gray White, Deborah. *Ar'n't I a Woman? Female Slaves in the Plantation South* (New York: W. W. Norton and Company, 1999).

25. Gray White, *Ar'n't I a Woman?*, p. 190.

26. Collins, Patricia Hill, *Black Feminist Thought: Knowledge, Consciousness, and the Politics of Empowerment* (New York: Routledge, 2000).

27. Collins, *Black Feminist Thought*, p. 26.

28. Gray White, *Ar'n't I a Woman?*; Stack, Carol, *All Our Kin* (New York: Basic Books, 1974).

29. Fernquist, "Education, Race/Ethnicity, Age, Sex, and Suicide"; Nisbet, "Protective Factors for Suicidal Black Females"; Taylor-Gibbs, Jewelle, "African American Suicide: A Cultural Paradox," *Suicide and Life-Threatening Behavior* 27 (1997): 68–79.

30. Ajrouch, Kristine J., Toni C. Antonucci, and Mary R. Janevic, "Social Networks among Blacks and Whites: The Interaction between Race and Age," *Journals of Gerontology Series B: Psychological Sciences and Social Sciences* 56 (2001): S112–S118.

31. Shattuck, Rachel M., and Rose M. Kreider, "Social and Economic Characteristics of Currently Unmarried Women with a Recent Birth: 2011," ed. USC Bureau (Washington, DC: American Community Survey Reports, 2013).

32. Fernquist, "Does Single Motherhood Protect against Black Female Suicide?"

33. Collins, *Black Feminist Thought*; Roberts, Dorothy, *Killing the Black Body: Race, Reproduction, and the Meaning of Liberty* (New York: Random House, 1997).

34. Fraser et al., "Social Support Choices for Help with Abusive Relationships."

35. Satcher, David, "Eliminate Disparities in Mental Health: A Report of the Surgeon General" (1999), http://www.cdc.gov/omhd/AMH/factsheets/mental.htm (accessed October 16, 2008); Smith, Elsie J., "Mental Health and Sevice Delivery Systems for Black Women," *Journal of Black Studies* 12, no. 2 (1981): 126–141; Wilson, Melba, "Black Women and Mental Health: Working towards Inclusive Mental Health Services," *Feminist Review* 68 (Summer 2001): 34–51.

36. Lewis-Harris and Davis-Molock, "Cultural Orientation, Family Cohesion, and Family Support in Suicide Ideation and Depression"; Griffin-Fennell and Williams, "Examining the Complexities of Suicidal Behavior in the African American Community"; Kaslow, Nadine J., Alissa Sherry, Kafi Bethea, and Sarah Wyckoff, "Social Risk and Protective Factors for Suicide Attempts in Low Income African American Men and Women," *Suicide and Life-Threatening Behavior* 35 (2005): 400–412; Taylor-Gibbs, "African American Suicide."

37. Lewis-Harris and Davis-Molock, "Cultural Orientation, Family Cohesion, and Family Support in Suicide Ideation and Depression."

38. Moynihan, *The Negro Family*; Rainwater and Yancey, *The Moynihan Report and the Politics of Controversy.*

## Chapter 5

1. Alisha, a respondent in the study, attributes black women's very low suicide rate to their resiliency. This quote is a response to my request to elaborate

on how the notion of strength and resiliency has impacted Alisha's perception of suicide.

2. Justine, a respondent in the study, offers her explanation for black women's low rate of suicide.

3. Center to Reduce Cancer Health Disparities, "Health Disparities Defined" (Rockville, MD: National Cancer Institute, 2007), http://crchd.cancer.gov/about/defined.html (accessed June 5, 2014); Collins, Patricia Hill, *Black Sexual Politics: African Americans, Gender, and the New Racism* (New York: Routledge, 2004); Sands, Aimee, "Never Meant to Survive, A Black Woman's Journey: An Interview with Evelyn Hammonds," in *Women, Science, and Technology: A Reader in the Feminist Science Studies*, ed. Mary Wyer, Donna Geisman, Hatice Orun Ozturk, and Marta Wayne (New York: Routledge, 2001), pp. 5–38; Sharpio, Thomas M., *The Hidden Cost of Being African American: How Wealth Perpetuates Inequality* (New York: Oxford University Press, 2004); Shorter-Gooden, Kumea, "Multiple Resistance Strategies: How African American Women Cope with Racism and Sexism," *Journal of Black Psychology* 30 (2004): 406–425; St. Jean, Yanick, and Joe R. Feagin, *Double Burden: Black Women and Everyday Racism* (New York: M. E. Sharpe, 1998); Staples, Robert, *The Black Woman in America* (Chicago: Nelson-Hall Publishers, 1973).

4. Adams, Z., and J. Simmons, "Black Women's Mental Health Issues," *Essence* 18 (1987): 77; Bhugra, Dinesh, and Oyedeji Ayonrinde, "Racism, Racial Life Events and Mental Ill Health," *Advances in Psychiatric Treatment* 7 (2001): 343–349; Moorer, Talise D., "Stress More Crippling in Black Women Than White Counterparts," *New York Amsterdam News* 97 (2006): 32–43; Nelson, Camille A., "Of Eggshells and Thin-Skulls: A Consideration of Racism-Related Mental Illness Impacting Black Women," *International Journal of Law and Psychiatry* 29 (2006): 112–136; Satcher, David, "Eliminate Disparities in Mental Health: A Report of the Surgeon General" (New Orleans: Center for Disease Control, 1999), http://www.cdc.gov/omhd/AMH/factsheets/mental.htm (accessed October 16, 2008).

5. Nora, Pierre, "Between Memory and History: Les Lieux de Mémoire," *Representations* 26 (1989): 7–24.

6. Collins, *Black Sexual Politics*; Gray White, Deborah, *Ar'n't I a Woman? Female Slaves in the Plantation South* (New York: W. W. Norton and Company, 1999); Deck, Alice, "Now Then—Who Said Chicken and Biscuits? The Black Woman Cook as a Fetish in American Advertising," in *Kitchen Culture in America: Popular Representations of Food, Gender, and Race*, ed. Sherrie A. Inness (Philadelphia: University of Pennsylvania Press, 2000) pp. 69–93.

7. Brown, Delindus R., and Wanda F. Anderson, "A Survey of the Black

Woman and the Persuasion Process: The Study of Strategies of Identification and Resistance," *Journal of Black Studies* 9 (1978): 233–248; Foster, Frances S., "Changing Concepts of the Black Woman," *Journal of Black Studies* 3 (1973): 433–454.

8. Thomas, Veronica G., "The Psychology of Black Women: Studying Women's Lives in Context," *Journal of Black Psychology* 30 (2004): 286.

9. Thomas, "The Psychology of Black Women," pp. 286–306.

10. Shorter-Gooden, "Multiple Resistance Strategies."

11. Mutua, Athena D., "Shifting Bottoms and Rotating Centers: Reflections on LatCrti III and the Black/White Paradigm," *University of Miami Law Review* 53 (1998–1999): 1177–1216.

12. Feagin, Joe R., *Racist America* (New York: Routledge, 2001).

13. Stack, Steven, "Suicide: A 15-Yr Review of the Sociological Literature Part I: Cultural and Economic Factors," *Suicide and Life-Threatening Behavior* 30, no. 2 (2000): 145–162.

14. Jones, Lani V., "Enhancing Psychosocial Competence among Black Women in College," *Social Work* 49, no. 1 (2004): 75–83.

15. Jones, Charisse, and Kumea Shorter-Gooden, *Shifting: The Double Lives of Black Women in America* (New York: HarperCollins, 2003).

16. Collins, *Black Sexual Politics*.

17. Deck, "Now Then—Who Said Chicken and Biscuits?"

18. Gray White, *Ar'n't I a Woman?*

19. Maekawa, Kikuo, "Production and Perception of 'Paralinguistic' Information," ISCA Archive, Proc. Speech Prosidy (March 2004): 1–8.

20. Bhugra, Dinesh, and Oyedeji Ayonrinde, "Racism, Racial Life Events and Mental Ill Health," *Advances in Psychiatric Treatment* 7 (2001): 343–349.

21. Crosby, Alex, and Sherry Molock, "Introduction: Suicidal Behaviors in the African American Community," *Journal of Black Psychology* 32 (2006): 253–261.

22. Centers for Disease Control and Prevention, "2011, United States Suicide Injury Deaths and Rates per 100,000," Web-based Injury Statistics Query and Reporting Sytem (WISQARS), September 2012, www.cdc.gov/injury/wisqars/index.html (accessed March 14, 2013).

23. McIntosh, Peggy, "White Privilege: Unpacking the Invisible Knapsack," in *Race, Class, and Gender in the United States*, ed. Paula S. Rothenberg (New York: Worth Publishers, 2010), pp. 172–177.

24. McIntosh, "White Privilege."

25. Feagin, *Racist America*.

26. Powell, John A., "The Racing of American Society: Race Functioning as a Verb before Signifying as a Noun," *Law and Inequality* 15 (1997): 99–125.

27. Powell, John, "Whites Will Be Whites: The Failure to Interrogate Racial Privilege," *San Francisco Law Review* 34 (2000): 419–464.

28. Kyndall, a respondent in the study, provides an explanation of the black-white suicide paradox. In this quote, I asked her to elaborate on why she believes white men's suicide rate exceeds black women's.

29. Feagin, *Racist America*.

## Chapter 6

1. Feagin, Joe R., and Melvin Sikes, *Living with Racism: The Black Middle-Class Experience* (Boston: Beacon Press, 1995), p. 1.

2. Brewer, Rose H., "Black Women in Poverty: Some Comments on Female-Headed Families," *Signs* 13 (1998): 331–339; St. Jean, Yanick, and Joe R. Feagin, *Double Burden: Black Women and Everyday Racism* (New York: M. E. Sharpe, 1998); Gray White, Deborah, *Ar'n't I a Woman? Female Slaves in the Plantation South* (New York: W. W. Norton and Company, 1999); Shorter-Gooden, Kumea, "Multiple Resistance Strategies: How African American Women Cope with Racism and Sexism," *Journal of Black Psychology* 30 (2004): 406–425; Belle, Deborah, and Joanne Doucet, "Poverty, Inequality, and Discrimination as Sources of Depression among U.S. Women," *Psychology of Women Quarterly* 27 (2003): 101–113.

3. Heilprin, John, "Oprah's Encounter with Racism Results in Apology from Swiss Tourism Office," HuffPost Black Voices, August 9, 2013, http://www.huffingtonpost.com/2013/08/09/oprah-racism-swiss-tourism-office_n_3731165.html (accessed November 15, 2013).

4. Henry, Alissa, "Black and Proud: Study Credits 'Positive Racial Regard' for Low Suicide Rate among Black Women," *Madam Noire* (2012), http://madamenoire.com/tag/black-womens-suicide-rate/ (accessed July 25, 2013).

5. Rockett, Ian, Julie Samora, and Jeffrey Coben, "The Black-White Suicide Paradox: Possible Effects of Misclassification," *Social Science and Medicine* 63 (2006): 2165–2175.

6. Brown, Delindus R., and Wanda F. Anderson, "A Survey of the Black Woman and the Persuasion Process: The Study of Strategies of Identification and Resistance," *Journal of Black Studies* 9, no. 2 (1978): 233–248; Collins, Patricia H., "The Social Construction of Black Feminist Thought," in *Gender and Scientific Authority*, ed. S. G. K. Barbara Laslett, Helen Longino, and Evelyn Hammonds (Chicago: University of Chicago Press, 1996); Jones, Charisse, and Kumea Shorter-Gooden, *Shifting: The Double Lives of Black Women in America* (New York: HarperCollins, 2003); St. Jean and Feagin, *Double Burden*; Stack, Carol,

*All Our Kin* (New York: Basic Books, 1974); West, Traci C., *Wounds of the Spirit: Black Women, Violence, and Resistance Ethics* (New York: New York University Press, 1999).

7. Stack, Steven, "Suicide: A 15-Yr Review of the Sociological Literature Part I: Cultural and Economic Factors," *Suicide and Life-Threatening Behavior* 30, no. 2 (2000): 145–162; Taylor-Gibbs, Jewelle, "African American Suicide: A Cultural Paradox," *Suicide and Life-Threatening Behavior* 27, no. 1 (1997): 68–79.

8. Alston, Maude H., and Sharon Eylar Anderson, "Suicidal Behavior in African American Women," in *Women and Suicidal Behavior*, ed. S. S. Canetto and D. Lester (New York: Springer Publishing Company, 1995), pp. 133–143; Durkheim, Émile, *Suicide* (London: Penguin, 1897); Fernquist, Robert M., "Does Single Motherhood Protect against Black Female Suicide?," *Archives of Suicide Research* 8, no. 2 (2004): 163–171; Kaslow, Nadine J., Carli H. Jacobs, Sharon L. Young, and Sarah Cook, "Suicidal Behavior among Low Income African American Women: A Comparison of First-Time and Repeat Suicide Attempters," *Journal of Black Psychology* 32, no. 3 (2006): 349–365; Lewis-Harris, Treniece, and Sherry Davis-Molock, "Cultural Orientation, Family Cohesion, and Family Support in Suicide Ideation and Depression among African American College Students," *Suicide and Life-Threatening Behavior* 30, no. 4 (2000): 341–353; Taylor-Gibbs, "African American Suicide."

9. St. Jean and Feagin, *Double Burden*.

10. Nisbet, Paul A., "Protective Factors for Suicidal Black Females," *Suicide and Life-Threatening Behavior* 26 (1996): 325–341.

11. Durkheim, *Suicide*; Neeleman, Jan, Simon Wessely, and Glyn Lewis, "Suicide Acceptability in African and White Americans: The Role of Religion," *Journal of Nervous and Mental Disease* 186, no. 1 (1998): 12–16; Taylor-Gibbs, "African American Suicide."

12. Walker, Rheeda L., David Lester, and Sean Joe, "Lay Theories of Suicide: An Examination of Culturally Relevant Suicide Beliefs and Attributions among African Americans and European Americans," *Journal of Black Psychology* 32 (2006): 320–334.

# Index

Achievement status, 11–12
Adaptation skills of black women, 92–95
African American experience, 7–8
Age: suicide rates for black and white males and females, 4
Aguirre, Adalberto, 22
*Ar'n't I a Woman* (Gray White), 68–69
Atheists, 17, 45–46, 50–51, 112
Attempted suicide, 4–5, 35–36, 39–40, 78–81, 108

Bearman, Peter, 11
Buddhists, 50
Burawoy, Michael, 15

Cancer, 5–6, 74
Caring for others, 30–33
Casual thoughts of suicide, 36–38, 108
Catholic Church, 50–52
Centers for Disease Control and Prevention (CDC), 38
Children and family: benefits of social support, 65–66; black women prioritizing God, 46–51; black women's connectedness, 111–112; black women's obligation to, 30–33; claims of weakening social networks in, 66–67; female-headed households, 22–23, 73; financial support for, 34–35; loss of family as stress factor, 39–40; motherhood as protective factor, 73074; as necessary support network, 79–81; as source of stress, 22, 43–44; suicide among family members, 37; suicide among whites, 95–96
Christianity. *See* Religious belief
Civil rights movement, strength derived from, 86
Civil War, 7–8
Collective life, 60
Collins, Patricia Hill, 14, 69
Coping strategies, 92–95
Crucifixion, 60
Cult of womanhood, 30

Deck, Alice, 91
Depression, 6–7, 23–24
Discrimination: food and ethnicity as apparatus of, 91–92; racing, 98–100; as risk factor, 79; from whites in public settings, 24–28. *See also* Oppression; Racism

135

Durkheim, Émile, 9–12, 60–61, 65–66

*Ebony* magazine, 30–31
Education: discrimination on campus, 25–27; suicide rates for black and white males and females, 4
Educational attainment, 6, 16–17
Ellison, Ralph, 29
Epidemiological data: completed suicide statistics, 3–5
Expectations of black women, 28–30, 88–89
Extended case method, 15

Faith. *See* Religious belief
Feagin, Joe, 27–28, 67, 89, 98, 111
Female-headed households, 22–23, 73
Financial want. *See* Poverty
Food as apparatus of discrimination, 91–92
Framework of respondents, 15
Fraser, Idelle, 65

Gender: dual discrimination against black women, 22–23, 67–68; Durkheim's theory of suicide, 10–11; gender stereotypes, 30; Hendin's theory of suicide, 13; racial and gender oppression, 8–9; shifting, 27; suicide attempts by race and, 4–5
Girard, Chris, 11–12
Gray White, Deborah, 14, 68, 92
Green, Vivian, 43–44

Hammonds, Evelyn, 68
Health and social disparities, 5–6, 23
Heart disease, 5–6
Hendin, Herbert, 12
Henry, Alissa, 105(quote), 107
Hierarchy of racial groups, 88
Hill, Robert, 66
Hopelessness, 77–79
Hurricane Katrina, 101

Ideations of suicide, 13, 38–40, 44, 51, 59, 84–85, 108
Identity: black women redefining themselves, 14; resulting from racial and gender oppression, 9; shifting, 27–28
Ideology: true womanhood, 30
Inequality: health and social disparities, 5–6; as source of stress, 24–25
Irish indentured servants, 7

Jezebel image of black women, 92
Jim Crow laws, 8
Joe, Sean, 46, 113
Jones, Charisse, 25, 27, 91, 94

Kilpatrick, Allie, 66

Lester, David, 46, 113
Lewis, Glyn, 60
Lumumba-Kasongo, Mana, 25

Maekawa, Kikuo, 92–93
Marital status: Durkheim's theory of suicide, 10–11
McIntosh, Peggy, 98
Mental health, 6–7, 14, 23–24, 75–76
Micro data, 15–16
Middle Passage, 85
Modernization, Prudhomme's theory of suicide and, 12
Moorer, Talise D., 7
Morality of suicide, 51–54
Moynihan, Patrick, 66
Muhammad, Shahida, 30–31
Murder, 59
Muslims, 48, 50
Mutually beneficial relationships, 111–112

Neeleman, Jan, 60

Oppression: history of struggle for black women, 109–110; internalization of cultural norms resulting from, 69–70; personal strength derived from, 86–89; social support stemming from, 63–64. *See also* Discrimination; Racism

Poverty and financial hardship: African American and white women, 22–23; black women's disproportional hardship, 34–35; black women's historical struggle with, 90–91; health and social disparities, 6; racism persisting through affluence, 106; as source of stress, 22; stereotypical portrayal of black women, 67; women as primary breadwinners, 34–35
Powell, John, 99
Probability of suicide, 97(fig.)
Protective factors. *See* Children and family; Religious belief; Social networks
Prudhomme, Charles, 12
Psychological well-being, social support and, 65–66
*The Psychology of Black Women: Studying Women's Lives in Context* (Thomas), 87–88

Race and ethnicity: the African American experience, 7–8; black women's view of the suicide paradox, 14–15; dual discrimination against black women, 22–23, 67–68; Durkheim's theory of suicide, 10–11; ethnicity as apparatus of discrimination, 91–92; explaining racial differences in suicide, 9–13; health and social disparities, 5–6; Hendin's theory of suicide, 13; shifting, 27; suicide rates for black and white males and females, 3–5
Racialized space, 99
Racing, 98–100
Racism: on campus, 26–27; consequences of racial and gender oppression, 8–9; powerlessness of black women, 67–68; unrealistic expectations placed on black women, 28–30
Reconstruction period, 7–8
Religious belief: black women prioritizing God, 46–51; black women redefining themselves as survivors, 14; black women's notions of faith, 19; black women's religious practices, 45–46; church attendance correlating with ethnic suicide rates, 44, 60–61; Durkheim's theory of suicide, 10; finding a higher purpose, 54–57; of interview participants, 17–18; promoting social integration, 64–65; sinful nature of suicide, 51–54; surrender stressors to God, 58–60; turning challenges into blessings, 43–44; unacceptability of suicide, 112–113
Research methodology: daily stressors, 108; failure to address black women's issues, 106–107; interview participants, 16–17; micro data and macro theory, 15–16; studying social connectedness, 115; working hypothesis, 17–18
Research results: black women's self-defined resiliency, 108, 110–111; implications for future research, 107–113; importance of faith, 112–113; importance of family, 111–112; managing long-term struggle, 109–110; suicidal thoughts and attempts, 108
Resiliency of black women, 83–84, 95, 108, 110–111
Risk factors: health and social disparities, 5–6; lack of social-network support, 77–81; mental health, 6–7. *See also* Stress factors

Safe spaces concept, 73
St. Jean, Yanick, 111
Sands, Aimee, 68

Scientific inquiry, 2–3
Segregation, 8–9
Selfishness, suicide as, 64, 71–72, 74
Self-perceptions of black women, 109–111
Serenity prayer, 58–59
Shifting, 27
Shorter-Gooden, Kumea, 25, 27, 46, 91, 94
Sikes, Melvin, 27–28
Sinful nature of suicide, 51–54
Slavery: the African American experience, 7–8; black women's long-term struggle, 109–111; development of women's social networks, 68–69; persistent legacy, 22; personal strength derived from, 85–87
Social activism, 63–64
Social connectedness: black women's obligations to family and friends, 30–33; faith-based beliefs and, 45; social support stemming from oppression, 63–64. *See also* Children and family
Social integration: benefits of social networks to black women, 64–66; Durkheim's theory of, 9–12, 18; family and religion promoting, 44–45, 51, 60–61, 64, 112; importance to black women, 65–66; role in suicide prevention, 69–70. *See also* Religious belief; Social networks
Social networks: advantage of close-knit communities, 19; benefits to black women, 64–66; black women's unyielding commitment to, 69–77; claims of weakening social networks in the black family, 66–67; lack of social-network support as risk factor, 77–81; positive reinforcement through, 74–77; research participants, 18; suicide among members of, 70; as vital survival tactic, 67–69. *See also* Children and family
Social position of black women, 66–67

Social regulation, 10
Socioeconomic status (SES) of interview participants, 16–17
Spiritual beliefs. *See* Religious belief
Statistics and demographics: attempted suicide, 5; interview participants, 16–17; suicide rates for black and white males and females, 1–5
Strength, personal: black women's adaptation skills, 92–95; black women's current social position, 87–89; black women's socioeconomic status, 89–91; current misrepresentations of black women, 91–92; explaining low suicide rates, 84–85; historical context and acquisition of, 85–87; origins of, 83–84; perception of weakness, 97–98; response to pressure, 100–103; suicide probability among white men and black women, 97(fig.); white males and black women, 94–95
Stress factors: black women's self-defined resiliency, 108; complexity of black women's lives, 105–106; consequences of the "strong black woman" myth, 30–33; depression, 23–24; discrimination from whites in public settings, 24–28; ideations of suicide, 38–40; of interview participants, 18; the pathological perspective, 13–14; poverty, 34–35; prejudice and discrimination, 21–22; religious life helping to navigate, 46; resilience stemming from, 83–84; surrendering problems to God, 58–60; unrealistic expectations placed on black women, 28–30. *See also* Risk factors
Stress management, 7
"Stress More Crippling in Black Women than White Counterparts" (Moorer), 7
Superwoman myth, 94

Theoretical explanations of racial differences in suicide, 9–13
Thomas, Veronica, 87–88
Thoughts of suicide. *See* Casual thoughts of suicide; Ideations of suicide
Turner, Jonathan, 22

Wage discrimination, 25–26
Walker, Rheeda, 46, 113
*Washington Post* survey, 31
Weakness, personal, 97–98, 97(fig.), 100–101. *See also* Strength, personal
Wessely, Simon, 60
West, Traci, 15–16, 67
White privilege, 88–89, 113–114; black women's perceptions of white men's suicide rates, 103(fig.); perception of weakness, 97–98; white men's response to pressure, 100–103
Winfrey, Oprah, 106
Womanhood in America, 30–33
Workplace, inequality as source of stress in, 24–26

## About the Author

**Kamesha Spates** earned her doctorate from Texas A&M University and is currently an assistant professor in the department of sociology at Kent State University. Her areas of specialization include the intersections of race, class, and gender; the African American experience; crime and deviance; and suicidology. Prior to joining the Kent State faculty she gained valuable teaching experience at Colorado State University–Pueblo and Blinn College. She also has extensive work experience in the areas of underrepresented-student retention and recruitment within higher education.